# JONATHAN EDWARDS

A Timeless Theologian
The History of Redemption (Period I)

A CELEBRATION OF FAITH SERIES

PAUL AURICH
JONATHAN EDWARDS

*To Karen, my beloved wife, who has faithfully
stood by my side for fifteen years*

~ Paul Aurich

www.cantaroinstitute.org

Published by Cántaro Publications, a publishing imprint of the Cántaro Institute, Jordan Station, ON.

Series Editor: Steven R. Martins
Book Design: Cántaro Institute

Library & Archives Canada
ISBN: 9781990771811

## ABOUT THE CÁNTARO INSTITUTE

*Inheriting, Informing, Inspiring*

The Cántaro Institute is a reformed evangelical organization committed to the advancement of the Christian worldview for the reformation and renewal of the church and culture.

We believe that as the Christian church returns to the fount of Scripture as her ultimate authority for all knowing and living, and wisely applies God's truth to every aspect of life, her missiological activity will result in not only the renewal of the human person but also the reformation of culture, an inevitable result when the true scope and nature of the gospel is made known and applied.

I am grateful for this contribution by Paul Aurich to the broader conversation that every Christian should be participating in about the redemptive work of God in all of history. Aurich's review and analysis of Jonathan Edwards' unfinished work, *The History of Redemption*, considers the work of the Triune God throughout time as He redeems Creation and brings all things into submission. In an era when discussions about the redemptive work of God are often limited to individual salvation, it is refreshing to step back and consider how God is at work through all of history, and in all of Creation, to fulfill his redemptive design, and to call his covenantal people to faithfully trust and participate in God's purposes now. I commend this work to every faithful Christian desirous of such a refreshing reminder in anticipation of the triumph of God over all created things.

— **Dr. Aaron Rock**
Lead Pastor, Harvest Bible Church
Fellow for Church Leadership, Ezra Institute

The scope of Jonathan Edwards' book, *A History of the Work of Redemption*, is extensive. As Paul Aurich notes, it could well be called his *magnum opus*. Edwards sets out to review the totality of God's redemptive work in history, from the Fall of man to the consummation of all things. Edwards' conclusion is that everything in human history from beginning to end stands in reference to the great work of redemption by Jesus Christ. Nothing can thwart Christ's redemptive work, and in the wisdom and sovereignty of God, all that comes to pass actually serves to advance it. In this valuable book, Aurich helps the reader recover the Biblical narrative of redemption from Genesis to Revelation as he takes the reader through Edwards' powerful book. It is breathtaking at times to consider the absolute sovereignty of God in controlling all of history for the purposes of his great work of redemption. Aurich also interacts with a number of current theological trends pointing out their deficiencies and lack of Biblical consistency and taking the reader back to Edwards and the Biblical text. The reader will be overwhelmed by a number of glorious theological truths. Spending time on these truths and other gems in this book will only expand the readers love and appreciation for the person and work of the Lord Jesus Christ. It may also convict many Christians whose view of God, his sovereignty and comprehensive plan of redemption are too small!

— **Jonathan Wellum**
President and CEO, Rocklinc Investment
Partners Inc.

# Table of Contents

**The History of Redemption:**
**Period I - From the Fall to the Incarnation**         79
*Jonathan Edwards*

# Series Preface

*What is faith? And why should we celebrate it?*

OF THE TWO QUESTIONS, the first is the most common, the second, on the other hand, is not given much thought, though it should logically follow. In our pluralistic world, the word "faith" has often been used as a token word for all forms of religious belief and expressions. You'll find it on bumper stickers, billboards, in a series of publications, even in film, music, media, you name it. Faith has somewhat become synonymous for "spirituality", which nowadays can mean almost anything. But is this *true* faith? That is, is this the true definition and understanding of faith, faith in the biblical sense of the term? The short answer is No. Not only does its definition fall short, its directional orientation is also off.

What then is faith? In order to understand what faith *is*, and what faith is *not*, we need to first understand the philosophical concepts of worldview and religion. These concepts, if based on biblical presuppositions, can help provide us with a logically consistent framework of thought, or the parameters by which we can answer these questions faithfully. Otherwise, we're faced with various conflicting definitions without any clear indication as to what is true.

Firstly, a *worldview* is what we all have, it is the lens by which we see the world and interpret its facts and evidences. There is not a single living and thinking person in the world who does not have a set of beliefs or presuppositions concerning reality. As a late apologist defined it, a "worldview" is:

> a network of presuppositions (which are not verified by the procedures of natural science) regarding reality (meta-physics), knowing (epistemology), and conduct (ethics) in terms of which every element of human experience is related and interpreted.[1]

Now, it goes without saying that not everyone's worldviews are correct. If one person believes that the earth is flat, and the other that the earth is round, and we mean in the same sense, only one of the two are right. But who? The two tests by which every worldview must be validated are the tests of logical consistency and correspondence. Is the worldview logically consistent? Does it correspond to reality? The Bible, as God's special revelation, provides us with the *true* worldview, a true set of presuppositions regarding reality, knowledge and ethics that are logically consistent and correspondent to reality. All other worldviews are antithetical to the true worldview and fail in the two tests of logical consistency and correspondence. Why? Because we live and breathe

1   Gary DeMar, ed., *Pushing the Antithesis: The Apologetic Methodology of Greg L. Bahnsen* (Powder Springs, GA.: American Vision Press, 2010), 42-43.

in God's world, and thus we can also say, because of the impossibility of the contrary.

Secondly, worldviews are not free and independent from *religion*. On the contrary, our worldview and religion are inseparable. The apostle James wrote to the church that "Religion that is pure and undefiled before God, the Father, is this: to visit orphans and widows in their affliction, and to keep oneself unstained from the world" (Jas. 1:27). In other words, *true* religion is to glorify God in all that we do, in every possible aspect of creational interaction and function – this includes administering the grace of the gospel – the result of consecrating the Lord as holy in the core essence of our being (1 Pet. 3:15). But just as there is *true* religion, as defined by God's special revelation, so there is *false* religion, that which is antithetical to the truth, expressed as worship of creation instead of the Creator (Rom. 1:25). To put it simply, our worldview is the *structure* of our presuppositions, what we believe to be true concerning reality, knowledge and ethics; while our religion is the *direction* of that respective structure, our worship; it is the underlying motive rooted in the condition of the human heart.

The reason that faith has been defined and understood in various ways is because it has been interpreted and expressed from a variety of different religious worldviews, all of which place an emphasis on faith's humanistic orientation (except for the Bible). And while it might seem that some elements of their understanding of faith contain a hint of truth, they are, as a whole system, in the wrong. Having then established the parameters by which we can answer our questions, that is, from the biblical religious worldview, what can we say then to What is faith? And Why should we celebrate it?

The term "faith" in the context of biblical Christianity is used in at least two distinct senses. According to *The Oxford Dictionary of the Christian Church*, it is firstly applied objectively to "the body of truth to be found in the Creeds, in the definitions of accredited Councils, in the teachings of doctors and saints, and, above all, in the revelation contained in the Bible."[2] It is, in other words, a term used to refer to the religious worldview of Christianity. Within this 'objective' faith, there is then, secondly, the 'subjective' faith, which Paul refers to in 1 Corinthians 13:13 as one of the three theological virtues alongside hope and love. *The Oxford Dictionary* explains that this faith "is the human response to Divine truth, inculcated in the Gospels as the childlike and trusting acceptance of the Kingdom [of God] and its demands, and known as 'the faith whereby belief is reached' (*fides qua creditor*)."[3] Whereas other religious worldviews would emphasize subjective faith as a natural human act, the Bible is clear in its teaching that faith is a supernatural act, that is to say, that a Christian can only have faith as a result of God's regenerative work in his heart (Ezek. 36:26-27; Jn. 1:12-13; 3:3-8; Tit. 3:5). To put

---

2  F.L. Cross, ed., *The Oxford Dictionary of the Christian Church*, second edition (Toronto, ON.: Oxford University Press, 1974), 499.

3  Ibid.

it simply, subjective faith is a gift from God for the objective faith of God's revealed truth.

Why must faith be an external gift? Because man, in his sin, cannot of his own volition turn to God in repentance and faith. His sinful disposition prevents this (Jn. 8:34; Rom. 6:20; 2 Tim. 2:25-26; Tit. 3:3). This is not to say that man cannot choose for himself between life and death (Deut. 30:15-20), it is rather that man's will is enslaved to his sinful nature and therefore cannot choose life, the life of Jesus Christ, unless he is first freed from this enslavement (2 Chron. 6:36; Job 14:4; Prov. 20:9; Eccl. 7:20; Jer. 13:23; Jn. 6:65). He will always want to choose death, because he is hostile to the truth of God (Gen. 6:5; Jn. 8:44; Rom. 1:18; 8:7-8; Eph. 4:17-19). This deliverance from his fallen condition is ultimately the work of the Spirit of God, who takes the heart of stone and replaces it with a heart of flesh (Ezek. 36:26), and having freed him from his captivity, with his renewed heart, he is then able to choose the only logical option before him, faith in the Lord and Saviour Jesus Christ and all that that entails (Acts 11:18; 13:48; Eph. 2:8-9; Phil. 1:29; 2 Tim. 2:25-26).

This is precisely why there are so many different religious worldviews in our day and age. Sin has not only caused our alienation from God and our spiritual death, it has also affected, or we might say "infected", the totality of our being, including our intellectual, mental faculties – what theologians call the *noetic* effects of sin. Instead of interpreting God's general revelation of creation as it truly is, by our fallen and hostile nature we supress the truth and devise for ourselves false world-views with inevitable god-substitutes (Rom. 1:18, 25). It is partly for this reason that God provided the special revelation of His word as the only authoritative inter-pretation of His created reality, for without it, we would be as blind men left with arms outstretched in the dark. But when God draws unto Himself men and women by his irresistible grace, these false god-substitutes are abandoned *by* faith *for* the true faith. As John Newton (1725-1807) wrote in his hymn *Amazing Grace*, "I once was lost, but now am found, was blind, but now I see."

If, therefore, faith that saves originates from God – for how else can man be saved? – then a celebration of faith is not only a celebration of what we believe, of what God has revealed – which should be celebrated in its own right – but what God has done to redeem sinful wretches such as ourselves. And what more reason do we need to celebrate faith than the fact that Christ has paid the ultimate sacrifice in order to save us from our fallen, sinful condition and the judgment that awaits the living and the dead (2 Tim. 4:1; 1 Pt. 4:5-6)? Not only does He rescue us from the darkness by forgiving us of our sin, having paid its penalty through his death (1 Cor. 6:20; Eph. 1:7; 1 Pt. 1:18-19; 1 Jn. 2:2; Rev. 5:9), He also reconciles us to the Father and begins the work of renewal and restoration, returning us, by the power of the Spirit and his sanctifying work, to our orig-inal state of righteousness and our creational purpose.

If our created purpose is, as *The Westminster Confession of Faith* states, to glorify God and delight in

Him forever (Rom. 11:36; 1 Cor. 10:31; Ps. 73:24-26; Jn. 17:22, 24), how can this at all be possible without faith? Does not the author of Hebrews write, "without faith it is impossible to please God"? (Heb. 11:6). It is for this reason also that we celebrate faith, for not only has God granted us the gift of saving faith, but faith makes it possible for us to fulfill our highest end, to glorify God and to delight in Him forever. To celebrate faith then is really to celebrate the glory of God, for true faith rooted in God's word only comes from God, the "author and finisher of our faith" (Heb. 12:2).

*A Celebration of Faith* is a series that reflects on the lives and contributions of those who have been touched by the grace of God, those who have professed, defended and advanced the Christian religious worldview. And while there are millions of stories to be told, the editorial team behind this series have sought to highlight some of the saints who have both inspired scores of generations towards living lives of faith, and others whose faith, although forgotten, have had a significant impact on the culture of their day. The purpose of this series is to inspire and encourage grace-bought believers towards living out their faith in such a way that demonstrates the truth, beauty and liberty of the gospel and its all-encompassing nature for the furtherance of God's kingdom.

Profiled in this volume is the eighteenth century American revivalist, philosopher, and theologian Jonathan Edwards (1703-1758), widely viewed as one of America's most original Christian thinkers. Edwards played an important role in the First Great Awakening

(1730s to 1740s), and the distinct school of theology he developed came to be known as New England theology. He wrote several sermons, including the classic *Sinners in the Hands of an Angry God*, and several books such as *The End for Which God Created the World*, and *The Life of David Brainerd*. It is no exaggeration to say that Edwards inspired thousands of missionaries by his ministry, and has no doubt inspired several leading Christian leaders in the present. The first volume of one of his greatest and final books, albeit not completed, *The History of Redemption*, has been included in this volume, preceded by a survey of Edward's theology written by Paul Aurich, a friend of the Cántaro Institute. Jonathan Edwards, the pastor, theologian, and missionary, credited as being one of the spiritual fathers of American evangelicalism, and widely read today by the church at large, stands as an exemplary figure of faith, worthy of being profiled in this series.

It is our hope that the Lord may use this book to help cultivate within the church a greater appreciation for our Christian heritage, for we inherit a great treasure in the faith that we have been bought into. May you be inspired through this profile to live out your faith boldly, undaunted by the challenges and afflictions of living in a fallen world, knowing that the Lord will sustain you as you seek to be the salt and light of the world (Matt. 5:13-16). And may you be equipped for, and informed as to the nature of the church's mission, to preserve and advance biblical truth, not only in its confession but also in its application, for the growth of God's kingdom and for His glory alone.

May God be glorified,
The Editorial Team
Cántaro Publications

# Edwards
## A Timeless Theologian

*Paul Aurich*

## 0.0 Introduction

CS LEWIS ONCE INSIGHTFULLY wrote that "the only pal-
liative is to keep the clean sea breeze of the centuries
blowing through our minds, and this can be done only
by reading old books."[1] Lewis identifies the problem of
only reading contemporary books without contemplating the time-tested wisdom of those who have gone before us. His words are a vivid reminder to the modern
Christian that truly hearing what classical authors have
to say is really about learning how to yield and submit
to God's creative wisdom which is particularly manifested by the brilliance of those who have gone before
us.[2] Modern Christians, though, have the tendency of
ensnaring themselves into the same assumptions as the

---

1   C.S. Lewis, *On the Incarnation.*
2   I am appreciative to Joshua Gibbs for this insight. He
mentions this idea in the introduction of his course, *Teaching
The Great* Books, a level one course, which is offered through
ClassicalU, https://www.classicalu.com/.

broader 'progressive' culture, which overvalues contemporary knowledge in the process of devaluing the time-tested wisdom of our Christian forbearers, who understood reality from the lens of a distinctly Christian worldview, where God's Word, as opposed to the broader culture, defines reality.

Hebrews 12:1-2 calls all Christians to "lay aside every weight and sin" by first, and for mostly "looking to Jesus, the founder and perfecter of our faith." But, in light of looking onto Jesus, the author of Hebrews also bids Christians to see that they stand amidst "a great cloud of witnesses." An acquaintance with Jonathan Edwards *(1703-1758)*, and his understanding of redemptive history would, thereby, serve modern Christians very well as his timeless classic, *The History of Redemption*, is certainly in keeping with Lewis' categorization of old books, which contemporary Christians should read and appreciate for themselves.

### 0.1 Edwards' Theological *Magnum Opus*

A *magnum opus* could be described as a significant achievement that tops all others within the portfolio of a writer's complete works. Edwards' work, *The History of Redemption*, though unfinished, could very well be his *magnum opus*. George Marsden, at least, believes this to be the case, when he observes that this work of Edwards is "the culmination of his life's work."[3] In keeping with his reformed and puritan tradition, Ed-

---

3  George Marsden, *Jonathan Edwards: A Life* (New Haven, CT: Yale University Press, 2003), 481.

wards confessed, in contrast to his humanistic contemporaries who asserted that man is the measure of all knowledge, that the Word of God is the final authority over every area of life. Edwards believed, in coordination with his reformed and puritan forebearers, that God, as opposed to man, is the final authority that grounds all truth claims. *The History of Redemption*, thereby, offers an understanding of redemptive history in faithful recognition of God's role as the transcendent sovereign over all truth.

Edwards clarified his intentions on writing *The History of Redemption* in an address that he made to the Princeton trustees in October 1757, stating:

> I have had on my mind and heart (which I long ago began, not with any view to publication) a great work, which I call *A History of the Work of Redemption*, a body of divinity in an entire new method, being thrown into the form of a history, *considering the affair of Christian theology, as the whole of it*, in each part, stands in reference to the great work of redemption by Jesus Christ; which I suppose is to be the grand design of all God's designs, and the *summum* and *ultimum* of all the divine operations and decrees; particularly considering all parts in the grand scheme in their historical order.

> This history will be carried on with regard to all three worlds, heaven, earth, and hell: considering the connected, successive events and alterations, in each so far as the Scriptures give any light; introducing all parts of divinity in that order which is most scriptural and most natural: which is a method which appears to me the most

> beautiful and entertaining, wherein every divine doctrine,
> will appear to greatest advantage in the brightest light,
> in the most off striking manner showing the admirable
> contexture and harmony of the whole.[4]

Edwards' address to the Princeton trustees articulately
captures his purpose in writing *The History of Redemption*. In composing this body of divinity, he wanted
to introduce a 'new method' in the form of history,
endeavoring to show how the events of all ages were
providentially ordered by God to promote the work of
redemption.[5] In Edwards' view, a comprehensive summary of Christian theology, articulated throughout the
entire span of human history was in order.[6] In this, Edwards purposed to capture what he called "the grand
design of all God's designs" to highlight the integral relationship between God's design in redemption and his
providential design of history. Edwards also mentions
the God-ordained stages in which the work of redemption would take place, being heaven, earth, and hell,
further demonstrating the transcendent and providential ordering of God's redemptive purpose, specifically
relating to eternity's past, the course of human history,
and the consummation of all things in Christ. Though

---

4  Edwards to Trustees of the College of New Jersey, October
1757, *Works*, 16: 727—28.

5  Edwards, *The History of Redemption*, 3.

6  Interestingly, *The History of Redemption* is based on a sermon
series, which Edwards preached in 1739, that focused on the
work of redemption in its entirety, beginning with eternity
past and culminating with the consummation of all creation in
Christ.

unfinished, *The History of Redemption* proves to be the summation of Edwards' life's work as he chronicles the comprehensive progress of redemption throughout the span of history.

## 0.2 The Need to Recover the Biblical Narrative of Redemption

A scriptural confession of redemptive history has been hindered by a modern form of Marcionism (an early church heresy), which has been permitted to fester within local churches, Christian organizations, and seminary settings. Wesley Hill, a contributor of *First Things,* describes Marcionism as "the belief that the Old Testament is not authoritative in matters of Christian doctrine and morals."[7] A reductionistic view of redemptive history that devalues God's preceding redemptive work, before Christ's incarnation, is the problematic outcome of such an understanding of the Old Testament. The default of modern Christians is to, thereby, understand the extent of redemption in terms of Christ's incarnation. This view of redemption sees Jesus as a revolutionary figure with the mandate to abolish 'old' and 'outdated' structures, which in their view, hinders the progress of the Kingdom of God. Andy Stanley, in his book *Irresistible*, typifies this popular view when he writes:

---

7  See "Andy Stanley's Modern Marcionism", *First Things*. Accessed August 19, 2021. https://www.firstthings.com/web-exclusives/2018/05/andy-stanleys-modern-marcionism/.

Jesus was new wine. Judaism and paganism were old wineskins. The new Jesus offered was a departure from the traditions of both. Jesus, along with his early followers, argued that Judaism and paganism both pointed to a day when God would unleash something new in the world, for the world. Those with eyes to see would recognize it. Those with ears to hear would listen and follow.

Specifically, Jesus came to establish a new covenant, a new command, and a new movement. His new movement would be international. The new covenant would fulfill and replace the behavioral, sacrifice-based systems reflected in just about every religion of the ancient world. His new command would serve as the governing behavioral ethic for members of his new movement.[8]

Stanley's portrayal of Jesus casts him in the light of the values of our 'out with the old and in with the new', broader culture. One would be remiss in accepting Stanley's words, here, as Christian. His presuppositions are progressive in every respect. The meaning behind the claim, that "Jesus is the new wine," carries with it the assumption that Jesus preached a message of never-ending progress, in the effort to deem the past as 'old.' The new covenant is, in Stanley's estimation, the dawning of a 'new international movement,' which, in his view, is the replacement of an old system, rooted in behaviour and sacrifice. Stanley, interestingly, puts the nation of Israel in the same category as pagan religions.

---

8  Andy Stanley, *Irresistible: Reclaiming The New That Jesus Unleashed for the World,* eBook version (Grand Rapids, MI: Zondervan, 2018) loc. 288-298.

Now to be sure, redemptive history is progressing. The church, for example, does not practice the ceremonial law as practiced by ancient Israel, because Jesus obeyed the entire law as the true covenant-keeping Israelite. The problem with Stanley's comments, here, is that they attempt to undermine God's work of redemption, which spans throughout the entire course of human history, resulting in a shallow view of the gospel and the Kingdom that sees the world in terms of possibilities as opposed to divine providence. Edwards, in contrast to Stanley, sees history in terms of the latter.

In reading *The History of Redemption*, it would be beneficial for Christians in the modern context to ask two questions: (i) How is Edwards' understanding of redemption different from the mindset of "Progressive Christianity"? And, in application to this previous question, (ii) How might we, in yielding to Edwards' understanding of redemption, cherish a Christo-centric view of history? Edwards would, in answer to the first question, depart from the modern portrayal of Jesus, which Stanley's position represents, by insisting that the incarnation of Jesus was one part (as important as that might be) of the grander design of redemptive history. Rooted upon Isaiah 58:8, a text, which I will later discuss, Edwards' central doctrinal assertions states, that "the work of redemption is a work which God carries on from the fall of man to the end of the world."[9] Edwards clearly understands from his reading of Scripture that the work of redemption in Christ defines the progress

9  Edwards, *The History of Redemption*, 5.

of history in its entirety. In this, Edwards is teaching us to abandon a reductionalistic theology that imprudently dismisses earlier parts of redemption as though the incarnation erases the historical significance of the moral law, the need for covenant keeping, and the institution of the ceremonial law. All the parts of redemptive history are important, precisely because redemptive history in its entirety is the design of the Triune God, planned in eternity, to promote the worship of the Godhead.

In answer to the second question, and in application to the first, Edwards vividly reminds us that Christ is the exclusive and primary agent, who has worked on behalf of his church, since the fall. If the work of redemption is one that began immediately after the fall, to be concluded at the closing of human history, then it is not unreasonable to conclude that Christ is the church's one advocate and redeemer. The Apostle Paul does state in 1 Tim 2:5 "For there is one God, and there is one mediator between God and men, the man Christ Jesus." Edwards, in affirming this truth, states at the offset:

> As soon as man fell, Christ entered on his mediatorial work. Then it was that he first began to execute the work and office of a Mediator. He had undertaken it before the world was made. He stood engaged with the Father from eternity to appear as man's Mediator, when there should be occasion: and now the time was come. When man fell, Christ immediately entered on his work, and actually took upon himself that office. Then Christ, the eternal Son of God, clothed himself with the mediatorial character, and therein presented himself before

the Father. He immediately stepped in between a holy, infinite, offended Majesty, and offended mankind, and was accepted in his interposition; and thus wrath was prevented from going forth in the full execution of that curse which man had brought upon himself.[10]

God's provision of Jesus Christ, who is appropriately the mediator of the church, because he is the mediator of all creation (Jn 1:13), has, therefore, been working on behalf of the church, since the fall. God's provisions of mercy throughout the Old Testament era were, according to Edwards and in contrast to modern-day Marcions, were accomplished by none other than Jesus Christ as he is the sole agent of mercy for the church. The redemptive goal of history, then, is Christo-centric in every respect.

This Introduction will, therefore, discuss Edwards' thinking on:

- The Three Distinct Periods of Redemptive History
- The Happiness of the Church and the Fate of her Enemies (Is 51:8)
- The Endurance of the Covenant of Grace and the Relationship between God's Righteousness and his Salvation
- Redemption taken 'more largely'
- The Design of Redemption

---

10   Ibid., 21.

## 0.3 The Three Distinct Periods of Redemptive History

Edwards argues that the accomplishment of redemption, which extends from the fall until the end of the world, divides into three distinct periods, extending from:

- The fall of man until the incarnation of Christ
- Christ's incarnation until his resurrection
- The resurrection until the end of the world

Since the chronological flow of redemptive history extends from the fall until the end of the world, in keeping with Edwards' main doctrinal statement, the division of redemptive history into these distinct periods is a very reasonable proposition on his part. Readers should, however, recognize that these three periods are not mutually exclusive as though they existed in their own right. The Triune God, through the providential duration of these three historical periods, accomplishes the work of redemption through the overall progress of his purpose in Christ Jesus.

## 0.4 The First Period: The Fall of Man Until the Incarnation of Christ

Through the first period, extending from the fall of man until the incarnation of Christ, God prepares for the incarnation of the Christ. Through the second period, Christ purchases the redemption of his church; and through the final period, extending from the resurrection until the end of the world, Christ gathers his church through the regenerative work of the Holy

Spirit. Edwards, therefore, understands the history of redemption within the context of a part to the whole framework. The work of redemption is one work, which has three distinct parts: (i) the preparation of Christ's coming, (ii) Christ's purchase of the elect, and (iii) the gathering of the elect through the regenerative work of the Holy Spirit.

Of course, in contemplating these three different parts of redemptive history, Edwards details the complex design of each of them. Edwards, by way of example, divides the first period into what he terms as "six lesser periods," which covers the entirety of Old Testament history. These six lesser periods are as follows:

- From the fall to the flood
- From the flood to the calling of Abraham
- From the calling of Abraham to Moses
- From Moses to David
- From David to the Babylonian captivity

While these lesser periods were unique in their own right (e.g., The period from the fall to the flood uniquely served a different purpose than the period that spanned between Moses and David), they did have one thing in common as they all prepared the way for the coming of the Christ. The Old Testament, having many different parts, did have unity, according to Edwards' understanding, in that each period uniquely prepared for Christ's coming. Edwards sums up the preparation of Christ's coming well as unifying feature of the Old

Testament when he writes:

> The great works of God in the world, during this whole space of time,[11] were all preparatory to this. There were many changes and revolutions in the world, but they were only the turning of the wheels of providence in order to make way for the coming of Christ, and what he was to do in the world. They were all pointed hither, and all issued here. Hither tended especially, all God's great works towards his church. The church was under various dispensations and various circumstances, before Christ came; but all these dispensations were to prepare the way for his coming. God wrought salvation for the souls of men through all that space of time, though the number was very small to what it was afterwards; and all his salvation was, as it were by way of anticipation. All the souls that were saved before Christ came, were only, as it were, the earnest of the future harvest.[12]

Edwards clearly understood the Old Testament period as anticipatory in the sense that the incarnation of Christ is the providential antecedent of all events recorded within the Old Testament Canaan. The accounts of salvation, where God triumphs over his enemies, while liberating his people to serve him in covenant faithfulness, serves as a foretaste of the grander reality, in which, Christ would fulfill God's grand purpose of redeeming the church and all creation with her. The Exodus, for example, where God delivers the Israelites through Moses from the clutches of Pharaoh,

---

11  The space of time, being from the fall to the incarnation.

12  Edwards, *The History of Redemption*, 19.

only to serve God in the promised land in covenant faithfulness, points us to Christ, who is the true redeemer of his church. The Exodus is anticipatory in the sense that, just as Moses delivered the nation of Israel from Pharaoh (God's enemy), so too, God would deliver his church from sin, the works of the devil, and the last enemy, death itself. For this reason, Edwards observes: "These salvations [meaning all of God's works of deliverance in the Old Testament] were all but so many images and forerunners of the great salvation Christ was to work out when he should come."[13] The first period then, chronicling the fall of man until the incarnation of Christ, was, in Edwards view, preparation for the incarnation of Jesus Christ.

## 0.5 The Second Period: Christ's Incarnation Until His Resurrection

The second period of redemption, which Edwards identifies, is the time between Christ's incarnation and resurrection. Though the timespan of this period is indeed the shortest of the three periods, covering only thirty-three years, Edwards highlights the fact of its significance, due to all that Christ accomplished during his humiliation as he observes:

> Though it was but between thirty and forty years, yet more was done in it than had been from the beginning of the world, to that time. We have observed, that all events, from the fall to the incarnation, were only preparatory for what was now done. And it may also be observed,

---

13   Ibid., 20.

that what was done before the commencement of time in the eternal counsels of God, and between the person's of the Trinity, chiefly respected this period.[14]

The period of Christ's humiliation was, according to Edwards, marked by all that Christ accomplished pertaining to redemption. Christ, thereby, accomplished all that the first period, between the fall until the incarnation, prepared, namely, as Edwards asserts, the "procuring and purchasing of redemption."[15] Edwards explains that Christ, in procuring and purchasing redemption, accomplished the work of redemption by his incarnation and the purchase itself. Edwards understood that the incarnation was essential to the purchase of redemption: if Christ did not take on human nature, and remained only in his divine state, the purchase of redemption would not have been possible. Of this, Edwards writes:

> I would consider Christ's taking upon him our nature to put himself in a capacity to purchase redemption for us—This was absolutely necessary, for though Christ, as God, was infinitely sufficient for the work, yet to his being in an immediate capacity for it, it was needful that he should not only be God, but man. If Christ had remained only in the divine nature, he could not have purchased our salvation; not from any imperfection of the divine nature, but by reason of its absolute and

---

14  Ibid., 197.
15  Ibid., 197.

infinite perfection: for Christ, merely as God, was not capable either of obedience or suffering.[16]

Edwards, here, insists on the critical importance of Christ's incarnation in the effort to achieve the overall work of redemption. The redeemed, before the incarnation and after the incarnation, needed a new representative, who would, in contrast to Adam, obey the scriptures perfectly. Christ, therefore, was the perfect candidate to add human nature to his divine nature. Had Christ remained in his divine state, as Edwards argues, the accomplishment of redemption would have been impossible, because Adam's disobedience necessitated a new representative, who would share in human nature and the divine nature. Edwards was, therefore, adamant on the point that the Christ's incarnation facilitated the purchase itself.

Of course, Edwards, in emphasising the critical importance of the incarnation, established the theological groundwork for the purchase of redemption through Christ's satisfaction and his merit. Edwards, then, in view of Christ's merit and his satisfaction, maintains that the purchase of redemption can either be taken strictly or more largely—strictly to only signify the merits of Christ, and largely to include both his merit and his satisfaction. In furthering explaining Christ's purchase of redemption, specifically relating to its parts, namely his merit and his satisfaction, Edwards goes on to write:

---

16  Ibid., 108.

> The word satisfaction is… sometimes used, to include not only propitiation, but also for his meritorious obedience. For, in some sense, not only suffering the penalty, but also obedience, is needful to satisfy the law. The reason of the various use of these terms seems to be, that they do not differ so much really as relatively. They both consist in paying a price of infinite value; but that price, as it respects a debt to be paid, is called satisfaction; and as it respects a benefit to be obtained, is called merit. He who lays down a price to pay a debt, does in some sense make a purchase; he purchased liberty from the obligation. And he who lays down a price to purchase a good, does as it were make satisfaction: he satisfies the conditional demands of him to whom he pays it. This may suffice concerning what is meant by the purchase of Christ.[17]

Satisfaction, according to Edwards, broadly refers to all that Christ accomplished during his earthly ministry to fulfill the requirements of the Father, namely propitiation and meritorious obedience (Deut. 4:1-3). As the God-man, the perfection of Christ's obedience defined his entire ministry. The church enjoys the inherent blessings that come with covenant obedience because Christ fulfilled all that God's law requires, thereby, qualifying him to be the righteous, wrath-bearing substitute, who would appease the Father by his one-time sacrifice (Heb. 10:14). Edwards, therefore, understood and recognized that the perfect fulfillment of God's law righteously brought about the satisfaction that the Father required for the full pardon of the church, "paying

---

17   Ibid., 209.

a price of infinite value." Satisfaction is the debt paid in full. But, as Edwards notes, the condition of the purchase also necessitates merit, a condition, which Christ also perfectly fulfilled as a hallmark of his earthly ministry. Edwards explains that merit respects a benefit to be obtained, which is the liberty of the Christian believer from the law's obligation that required perfect obedience from them, a requirement that no one, apart from Christ, is capable of fulfilling. Edwards, then, in explaining the second period of redemptive history, highlights both Christ's incarnation and his purchase of the church as hallmarks of the grand design of the Trinity in restoring all creation to its pre-fallen state with Christ as creation's head and mediator.

## 0.6 The Third Period: The Resurrection Until the End of the World

The era of the Spirit, where the Kingdom of God advances through the regenerative growth of the church is, according to Edwards, the third period of redemptive history. Edwards' main doctrinal assertion states that the third period is "the space of time from the resurrection of Christ to the end of the world… all engaged in bringing about the… success, of Christ's purchase."[18] The growth and advancement of the church is, thereby, in Edwards' view, the hallmark of the third period of redemptive history. The Spirit's work to sanctify the people of God in Christ Jesus is the vivid mark of the success that Christ gained through the work of his in-

---

18  Ibid., 244.

carnation and purchase: the righteousness of his satisfaction and his merit ushered in the reign of Christ's
eternal Kingdom on earth.

Edwards insightfully identifies the institution of the
third period, because of the success of Christ's incarnation and purchase, as the ending of Satan's visible
kingdom, and inauguration of Christ's eternal Kingdom.
The temporal world, which is coming to an end, is,
in Edwards' view, the cessation of carnal ordinances.
Edwards writes:

> The *carnal ordinances of the Jewish worship* came to an
> end, to make way for the establishment of that spiritual
> worship, the worship of the heart, which is to endure to
> eternity; 'Jesus saith unto the woman, Believe me, the
> hour cometh, when ye shall neither in this mountain,
> nor yet at Jerusalem, worship the Father — But the hour
> cometh, and now is, when the true worshippers shall
> worship the Father in spirit and in truth; for the Father
> seeketh such to worship him," John 4:21-23. This is one
> instance of the temporal world's coming to an end, and
> the eternal world's beginning. Another instance is, that
> *the outward temple*, and the city of Jerusalem, came to
> an end, to give place to the setting up of the spiritual
> temple and the city, which are to endure forever; which
> is also another instance of removing those things which
> are ready to vanish away, that those things which cannot
> be shaken may remain. Again, *the old heathen empire*
> comes to an end, to make way for the everlasting empire
> of Christ. Upon the fall of antichrist, an end will be put
> to Satan's visible kingdom on earth, to establish Christ's

eternal kingdom; 'And the Kingdom and dominion, and the greatness of the Kingdom under the whole heaven, shall be given to the people of the saints of the most High, whose kingdom is an everlasting kingdom, and all dominions shall serve and obey him," Dan 7:27 which is another instance of the ending of the temporary world, and the beginning of the eternal one. And then, lastly, the *very frame of this corruptible world* shall come to an end, which shall last to eternity.[19]

Here, Edwards highlights four instances where the temporal world is passing away only to be replaced by a greater state of things, another hallmark of Christ's perfect obedience. In the first instance, as Edwards explains, God abolished the ordinances of Jewish worship to make way for the eternal worship, empowered by the Spirit of God, which Christ obediently secured by his incarnation and purchase. In the second instance, Edwards observes that God replaced the outward temple and the city of Jerusalem with the eternal temple, which is the living church, where Christ is the cornerstone. Edwards then goes on to explain the third instance, where God replaces the old heathen empires with the empire of Christ through the regeneration of the church: in this sense, we might rightly conclude that the Kingdom of God is imperialistic in every way, due to the victory of Christ, the victory on which the entirety of history appropriately pivots. The final instance of replacement, which Edwards identifies as the very frame of this corruptible world, is that we, the cor-

---

19   Ibid., 247-48.

ruptible, will be rendered incorruptible (1 Cor 15:53).[20] Like Christ's resurrected body, the corruptibility of creation will supernaturally become uncorrupted because of the success of Christ's incarnation and purchase. The institution of the third period, then, marks, in Edwards' mind, the ending of the temporal structures, destined to pass away for the eternal structures, which Christ established by the perfection of his obedience.

Edwards thinking, thus, maintains that the universal reign of Christ is the purpose and end of both creation's design and the span of history for that matter. He writes,

> The end of God's creating the world was to prepare a kingdom for his Son (for he is appointed heir of the world), and that he might have the possession of it, and a kingdom in it, which should remain to all eternity.[21]

Edwards recognizes that the temporary structures of the nations were always meant to be temporary, so that Christ would be vividly seen as the conquering king, who would establish his reign, once he had conquered his enemies. The advancement of the church throughout

---

20  In saying this, one must not assume that Edwards is referring to the destruction of creation. Edwards would reject such an assumption, due to the fact that he cherished a high view of creation. Moreover, as I will shortly discuss, Edwards maintains that the preparation of a Kingdom for God's Son is the purpose behind creation. The relationship between the reign of Christ and the goodness of creation is the basis for the eternal endurance of the physical world, contrasting the gnostic assumption that idealizes the spiritual realm and brings undue contempt upon the physical realm.

21  Ibid., 249.

the nations, during the third period of redemptive history, reminds us of the certainty, not only of Christ's success during his earthly ministry, but also Christ's success in gathering a covenant people for his own from every nation and tongue.

Edwards' understanding of the church age stresses the advancement of the Kingdom of God as the mark of Christ's success during his earthly ministry. The norm of the time between Christ's resurrection and his second coming is, in Edwards' view, the establishment of the kingdom of God on earth in preparation for the full disclosure of the reality that marks our current era of history, Christ's present reign as evidenced by the advancement of the church throughout the nations. Edwards writes:

> This kingdom of heaven is the evangelical state of things in his church and in the world, wherein consists the success of Christ's redemption in this period. There had been often great kingdoms set up before. But Christ came to set up the last kingdom, which is not an earthly kingdom, but a heavenly, and so is properly called the Kingdom of heaven.[22]

Here, we see Edwards' outlook on the eternal nature of Christ's Kingdom. The success of both Christ's incarnation and purchase ushered in the period, where Christ would establish his kingdom in the present, which will endure for all eternity. Edwards, for this reason, calls the reign of Christ, 'the last kingdom.' Christ's victory,

---

22  Ibid., 250.

while on earth, established the church's advancement in the present age. The reality of Christ and his conquest over all nations is realized by what Edwards terms as 'the evangelical state of things in the church and the world,' confirming Christ's words to Pilate, "My kingdom is not of this world" (Jn. 18:36).

## 0.7 The Happiness of the Church and the Fate of her Enemies (Isa. 51:8)

The theological credibility of sound doctrine exclusively rests, not on a collective agreement on the interpretation of a particular text, but on one's unwavering and unyielding obedience to the transcendent truths revealed in God's Word: his inscripturated, creational, and incarnational Word, and must, thereby, be the starting point of all forms of theological discourse. The timelessness of Edwards' insights, in his theological masterpiece, *The History of Redemption*, is one of many of his written manifestations of his uncompromising faithfulness to the Word of God. Readers of *The History of Redemption*, would do well to start with the following two questions: What is the biblical appeal that grounds Edwards' doctrine of redemption? And keeping this initial question in mind, How does Edwards differentiate between the happiness of the church and the fate of her enemies?

In answer to the *first question*, Edwards' biblical anchor, in *The History of Redemption*, interestingly starts with Isaiah 51:8, which, highlights the stark contrast between the happiness of the church and the fate of her enemies: "For the moth will eat them up like a garment, and the worm will eat them like wool, but my righteousness will be forever, and my salvation to all generations" (Isa. 51:8), thereby, reminds us that the Triune God is the great comforter of his church, bringing to mind his promised salvation, and with this, the deliverance from her enemies. Edwards' application of this text, thereby, gives the people of God reason to stalk confidence in the reliability of the redemptive promise of the salvation, which is in Christ Jesus.

In answer to the *second question* on how Edwards differentiates between the happiness of the church and the fate of her enemies, he makes two thoughtful observations from his reading of Isaiah 52:8.

*First of all,* Edwards observes that the power and prosperity of the church's enemies is *only* temporary, appealing to the opening line of the text, "For the moth will eat them up like a garment, and the worm will eat them like wool." This text brings to mind the hope, that even though unbelievers might appear to enjoy wealth and prosperity in the moment, their stubborn refusal to obey the Word of God will eventually lead them down the path to eternal ruin. This is in keeping with Psalm 73:18, which states, "Truly you set them in slippery places; you make them fall to ruin. How they are destroyed in a moment, swept away utterly by terrors" (ESV). Edwards does, in fact, highlight the vain and temporal hopes of the church's enemies, in no shortage of vivid terms, revealing their eventual end, which will suddenly come upon them. Edwards writes:

> However great their (the enemies of the church's) pros-
> perity, and however great their present glory, they shall
> by degrees consume and vanish away by a secret curse
> of God, till they come to nothing; and their power and
> glory, and consequently their persecutions, eternally
> cease; and themselves be finally and irrecoverably ruined:
> as the finest and most glorious apparel will in time wear
> away, and be consumed by moth and rottenness. We
> learn who those are that shall thus consume away, by
> the foregoing verse, namely, those that are the enemies
> of God's people.[23]

This description of the end, that will eventually come
upon the enemies of the church, is a vivid revelation of
Edwards' outlook on the inevitable outcome of those
who persist in unbelief in opposing the church— "they
will come to nothing," being "under the secret curse of
God." Such grim descriptions highlights Edwards' outlook on those who unrepentantly persist in violating
God's Word, based on his faithful observation of this
biblical text, which is a confirmation to the church that
the lawlessness of persecution will eventually come to
an end within the grandular scope of God's providence
and timing. Edwards, thereby, encourages Christians
to cherish the truth that the church's hope is in the
righteousness of God.

## 0.8 The Happy Lot of the Church's Eternal Inheritance

*Secondly*, the church, as Edwards maintains, will inherit "a happy lot and portion" as they are the people in

---

23  Ibid., 2.

whom the law of God resides. This, of course, is his appeal to the second part of Isaiah 51:8, "but my righteousness will be forever, and my salvation to all generations." Edwards, in initially grounding his doctrine on redemption as it relates to God's righteousness, pinpoints the stark contrast that exists between the church, who has reason to take comfort in the righteousness of God, and her enemies, who's power and glory, as already mentioned, will eventually come to nothing. Edwards observes:

> The contrary happy lot and portion of God's church, is expressed in these words, "My righteousness shall be for ever, and my salvation from generation to generation." Also who those are that shall have the benefit of this, by the preceding verse, namely, They that know righteousness, and the people in whose heart is God's law;" or, in one word, the church of God.[24]

Here, Edwards points out that the church's inheritance, and her happy state in Christ, unlike that of her enemies, is guarded because of his righteousness. The people of God will, thereby, forever delight in God's salvation, which is the constant and the hope of redemptive history. Yet, Edwards, in highlighting this hope in the righteousness of God, identifies the true state of the church, which is also the product of the righteousness of God, being those, who know the righteousness, and thereby, love his law.

---

24  Ibid., 2.

## 0.9 The Endurance of the Covenant of Grace and the Relationship Between God's Righteousness and His Salvation

Isaiah 51:8, thereby, gave Edwards reason to understand salvation within the grander context of the righteousness of God. Edwards, thus, maintained, in accordance with the scriptures, that the church's confidence in their salvation rested solely upon the righteousness of God in Christ, which is the hallmark of the covenant of grace, raising the questions: What is the relationship between God's righteousness and His salvation? And how does this inform Edwards' understanding of the endurance of the covenant of grace? In *answer to these questions,* Edwards would undoubtably direct attention to the fact that the righteousness of God is the *cause* of salvation.

## 0.10 The Righteousness of God as the Cause of Salvation

Edwards maintains that the righteousness of God, as understood from Isaiah 51:8, is his divine purpose to fulfill his covenant promise to his church. The church's security, by implication, thereby, rests upon God's unyielding commitment to keep his Word— "if we are faithless, he remains faithful." (2 Tim. 2:13). Edwards writes:

> By God's righteousness here, is meant his faithfulness in fulfilling his covenant promises to his church, or, his faithfulness towards his church and people, in bestowing the benefits of the covenant of grace upon them; which

benefits, though they are bestowed of free and sovereign grace, and are altogether undeserved; yet as God has been pleased, by the promises of the covenant of grace, to bind himself to bestow them, so they are bestowed in the exercise of God's righteousness or justice.[25]

God's faithfulness in fulfilling his covenant is, as Edwards observes, the outcome of his righteousness. The church has consistently enjoyed the benefits of sovereign grace throughout the span of redemptive history because all that God offers the redeemed in Christ is done so on the standard of God's righteousness. Since God will never forsake his righteousness, the people of God rest in the confidence that God will fulfill his righteousness through their salvation.

Edwards, of course, in purposing to establish his theological understanding on the righteousness of God as it relates to the salvation of the church, grounds his doctrinal confession on the Word of God. 1 John 1:9, for instance, is one text that Edwards appeals to, which grounds the biblical credibility of his argument: "If we confess our sins, he is faithful and just to forgive us our sins and to cleanse us from all unrighteousness." The Apostle John, in writing this, grounds his hope, of the believers' capacity to confess his sins and to be forgiven, upon God's faithfulness and justice. Furthermore, Daniel 9:16 attributes the Lord turning away his wrath from Jerusalem, to that which accords with his righteousness, stating "O Lord, according to all your righteous acts, let your anger and your wrath turn away from your

---

25  Ibid., 2.

city Jerusalem, your holy hill, because for our sins, and for the iniquities of our fathers, Jerusalem and your people have become a byword among all who are around us." Here again, we see Edwards' theology, on the righteousness of God as it relates to the salvation of the church, confirmed by the biblical witness as evidenced in Daniel's writings: God, indeed, brings salvation to his people in accordance with his righteousness. God is saviour and will save to the uttermost because he is righteous (cf. Heb. 6:10, Neh. 9:8, Ps. 36:10, 51:14).

The salvation of the church with all creation with it, then, is the outcome of God's righteousness. The righteousness of God and the salvation of his people go hand in hand. Edwards writes:

> God's righteousness and his salvation, the one is the cause, of which the other is the effect. God's righteousness or covenant of mercy is the root, of which his salvation is the fruit. Both of them relate to the covenant of grace. The one is God's covenant of mercy and faithfulness, the other intends that work by which this covenant mercy is accomplished. For salvation is the sum of all those works of God, by which the benefits of the covenant of grace are procured and bestowed.[26]

Edwards employs the imagery of the fruit that comes from the root to highlight the necessary relationship that exists between the righteousness of God with the salvation of the church. He compares God's righteousness with the root, and salvation with the fruit. Just as

---

26  Ibid., 3.

the root of a tree is essential for its existence, and the growth of the fruit it produces, so too, the righteousness of God is essential for the salvation of the church. God's faithfulness in keeping his covenant promise, as already mentioned, is the necessary condition for both the procurement and the bestowment of the covenant of grace.

## 0.11 The Historical Duration of the Covenant of Grace

God's determined purpose for redemptive history will come to fruition in accordance with his providence and design — this is what is meant behind the meaning of 'from generation to generation' in Isaiah 51:8. Edwards, in discussing the various biblically grounded meanings that come from phrases like, 'from generation to generation,' observes that the Bible does, in various places, refer to 'as long as man lives.' He also stresses that this phrase can be taken in a *limited sense*, specifically signifying Christ work of redemption, which began and finished with the duration of his humiliation. Many Christians do fall on the assumption that the work of redemption is limited to the incarnation. On this matter Edwards writes:

> Here it may be observed, that the work of redemption is sometimes to be taken in a limited sense, for the purchase of salvation, for so the word strictly signifies, a purchase of deliverance; and if we take it in this sense, the work of redemption was not so long in doing: but it was begun and finished with Christ's humiliation. It was begun with Christ's incarnation, carried on through

his life, and finished with his death, or the time of his remaining under the power of death, which ended in his resurrection: and so we say, that the day of Christ's resurrection is the day when he finished the work of redemption, that is, then the purchase was finished: and the work itself, and all that appertained to it, was virtually done, but not actually.[27]

Edwards is clearly not denying the importance of understanding redemption in this limited sense. Christ, during his incarnation, did purchase the redemption for his saints through his active and passive obedience, while on earth, but Edwards, in saying this, alludes to a grander understanding, where "redemption is taken more largely." This grander understanding of redemption, which Edwards himself adheres to, stresses that the duration of redemptive history extends from the first generation to the last generation, where man lives under the bondage of the curse. Edwards observes:

This expression, 'from generation to generation,' may determine us, as to the time which God continues to carry on the work of salvation for his church, both with respect to the beginning and the end. It is from generation to generation, that is throughout all generations; beginning with the first generation of men upon the earth, and not ending till these generations end, with the world itself.[28]

Here, Edwards maintains that the phrase 'from genera-

---

27  Ibid., 6.
28  Ibid., 4.

tion to generation,' refers to the chronology, being the timespan between the fall and the end of the world, in which God works to gather his people from the ends of the Earth. So, redemption is Christ's active and passive obedience while on earth, but redemption is also God's work of preparing the way for Christ's coming through the Old Testament offices of prophet, priest, and king. God's work of redemption also encompasses the church age, where God, by the regenerative power of the Holy Spirit, gathers the church out from the nations to be his cherished possession. Edwards' insights on redemption, taken more largely, is an encouragement for modern Christians to adopt a more comprehensive confession of redemption, which informs all reality. Since God's purpose to redeem the church, in Christ by the Spirit, is the one constant of history, believers in Christ have a foundational reason to affirm the truth that God's work of redemption spans generations (cf. Ecc. 1:4, Jn. 6:51), yielding the fruit of righteousness in the lives of Christian believers, which will not perish, well into eternity.

## 0.12 Redemption Taken "More Largely"

Christians, in the modern church, commonly resort to the assumption that redemption is to be understood in a *limited sense*, that is to say, Christ's work on earth, during the incarnation. Now to be sure, Christ, in purchasing the redeemed through his life, death, and resurrection, is certainly an integral part of the redemptive process, but Christians run into reductionism when the incarnation of Christ is viewed as redemption in its entirety. Edwards urges his readers to understand that, though Christ's redemptive work is to properly be appreciated in a limited sense, the gospel account of his life, death, and resurrection must be seen as one important part within the metanarrative of redemptive history. In this sense, Edwards' writing challenges Christians to think deeply about redemptive history.

Redemption, *taken more largely*, as Edwards puts it, sees the timeframe for purchasing the church from the grips of sin as taking place over the *entire* course of history. In fact, one might correctly argue that the redemption of the church is the very reason and purpose for existence and the course of history. The incarnation of Jesus Christ is, indeed, a critical juncture in the span of redemptive history, but, if one only gives exclusive attention to Christ's specific work of redemption without seeing his active and passive obedience within the broader context of redemptive history, a reductionistic understanding of redemption will be the inevitable result, begging the question, how does Edwards define redemption as it relates to being taken *'more largely'*? If Edwards were asked this question, the following excerpt might broadly be a way in which he would answer:

> Sometimes the work of redemption is taken more largely, as including all that God doth tending to this end; not only the purchase itself, but also all to this end; not only the purchase itself, but also all God's works that were properly preparatory to, or applicatory of, the purchase, and accomplishing the success of it: so then the whole dispensation, as it includes the preparation, the purchase,

and accomplishing to, or applicatory of, the purchase, and accomplishing the success of it: so then the whole dispensation, as it includes the preparation, the purchase, and the application and success of Christ's redemption, may be called the work of redemption. All that Christ does in this great affair as Mediator, in any of his offices, either of Prophet, Priest, or King; either when he was in this world in his human nature, or before, or since: and not only what Christ the Mediator has done, but also what the Father or the Holy Ghost have done, as covenanted in this design of redeeming sinful men; or, in one word, all that is wrought in execution of the eternal covenant of redemption; this is what I call the work of redemption in the doctrine: for it is all but one work, one design. The various dispensations or works that belong to it, are but the several parts of one scheme. It is but one design that is formed, to which all the offices of Christ directly tend; in which all the persons of the Trinity conspire; and all the various dispensations that belong it are united. The several wheels are one machine, to answer one end, and produce one effect.[29]

Edwards explains, in this excerpt, the comprehensive scope of redemptive history, spanning from the fall to the end of the world, grounding the central argument of *The History of Redemption*, which asserts, "the work of redemption is a work which God carries on from the fall of man to the end of the world."[30] He observes that the accomplishment of redemption, which will fi-

---

29  Ibid., 6-7.
30  Ibid., 4.

nally be realized at the end of the world, would see the gradual fulfillment of three successive dispensations, covering the entire span of history, the *first*, being the Old Testament, which is the period of preparation — the *second* period being Christ's incarnation, which is the period of purchase, and *finally* the *third*, being the church age or the age of the Spirit, which is the accomplishment or success of redemption. Here, we see Edwards' initial discussion on Christ's mediatory office, where he perfectly fulfills the offices of prophet, priest, and king, not just during his incarnation, but also in his preincarnate state. But it is also noteworthy to consider Edwards' thinking on the agency of all three members of the Trinity in the grand design of redemption. He recognizes that both the Father and the Holy Spirit also work, in harmonious co-ordination with Christ, in the execution of redeeming sinful men out from the world into the company of the church. Edwards, therefore, argues that redemption is 'but one design,' having various dispensations, but in all of which Christ's offices relate. Edwards draws us to cherish a holistic understanding of redemption, where the incarnation of Christ is one part of the grand design of the redemptive purpose, that the Triune God providentially designed in eternity.

## 0.13 The Meaning of Redemption

Edwards' spirit and firm conviction to conform all of his thinking and writing under the tutelage of God's Word enabled him to grasp a robust understanding of redemption, which, in turn, illumined his understanding of its meaning. Many within the modern church, being quite content with focusing attention on practicality, find themselves preoccupied with the here and now while the theological depth of redemptive history is ignored as nothing more than an afterthought. But Edwards, not being modernistic in his thinking, meticulously dedicated his thinking and writing to contemplating the full meaning of redemption, rooted in the inspiration of God's inerrant and authoritative Word. The modern church would, indeed, do well to learn from Edwards, as one who has come before us (Heb. 12:1-2). The meaning of redemption in accordance with the scriptures, begs the question: How does Edwards convey his understanding of redemption, and its meaning, in the effort to help Christians appreciate God's grand design in seeing all of his redemptive purposes come to fulfillment? Edwards' would answer this question by highlighting God's *providential design in redemption*, and the *effects of redemption*, specifically relating to the souls of the redeemed, as well as the grand design in general.

## 0.14 God's Providential Design in Redemption

The timeframe of God's redemptive purposes, as previously mentioned, is not limited to the work that Christ accomplished during his incarnation, important as this is. Interestingly, the timeframe of God's redemptive purposes is not even limited to the events that proceeded the fall. The timeline of God's providential purposes in redemption extends well before the fall into eternity's past with the set purpose of bearing fruit in the time from the fall 'til the consummation, when all things in creation will be united in Christ. Certainly, Edwards maintains that the timeframe of God's redemptive purposes, which can also be called his providence, was not limited to the events proceeding the fall. For Edwards, God's purpose to bring about redemption was not a novel reaction to Adam's disobedience. God's providential design to bring about the redemption of the saints originated from the mind of God in eternity past, realized through the dispensations of redemptive history, where Christ serves as the church's advocate and mediator until the end of human history, where the fruits of redemption will be the eternal reward of Christ's obedience.

God, thereby, orchestrated the events of redemption to culminate in the final disclosure of Christ's eternal Kingdom. Of this, Edwards writes,

> when it is said, that the work of redemption is carried on from the fall of man to the end of the world, it is not meant, all that ever was done... has been done since the fall.[31]

Edwards, here, is ruling out any perceived notions that redemption or the redemptive process is novel to the events of the fall. The fall did indeed witness the initiation of God's redemptive purposes as he noticeably prepared for Christ's incarnation (Gen 3:15), but the events of the fall, as Edwards observes, did not catch

---

31  Ibid., 8.

God's creational purpose off guard as though redemption was a contingency plan. Edwards very clearly maintained that redemption was and is a creational ordinance, harmoniously planned by the Triune God in eternity, and harmoniously enacted through the advent of God's providential purposes.

Edwards did observe that God was working for the purpose of redemption before he established creation. Redemption, according to Edwards, is not to be viewed as God's afterthought in response to the fall. The members of the Trinity, thereby, harmoniously planned redemption as a creational ordinance, which would yield eternal results. Edwards writes:

> Some things were done before the world was created, yea, from all eternity. The persons of the Trinity were, as it were, confederated in a design, and a covenant of redemption; in which covenant the Father had appointed the Son, and the Son had undertaken the work; and all things to be accomplished in the work were stipulated and agreed: and besides these, there are things done at the creation of the world, in order to that work, before man fell; for the world itself seems to have been created in order to it. The work of creation was in order to God's works of providence; so that if it be inquired, which of these are the greatest, the works of creation, or the works of providence? I answer, the works of providence; because God's works of providence are the end of his work of creation; as the building a house, or the forming an engine

or machine, is for its future use. But God's main work of providence is this great work of redemption.[32]

Here, we learn that the process of redemption is, in Edwards' view, not limited to the present continuum of time and space, meaning that God's planning of redemption, is not conditioned upon the temporal event of the fall. Edwards highlights the harmony that pre-existed among the Godhead before the world was created. The members of the Trinity, as Edwards observes, collaborated in the design of redemption. The Father commissioned the son to undertake the work of redemption, and the son, in accordance with the Father's predetermined purpose, agreed to accomplish the preparation, the purchasing, and the gathering of his church, set apart from the world. Redemption in Christ Jesus, as Edwards notes is thereby the chief end of God's providential design for this world. One might correctly conclude from Edwards' thinking here that the existence of creation, being the outcome of God's providential design – that it's design with all of its diversity – was spoken into being to fulfill God's established plan of redemption. Every area of Creation, then, exists and has being in order to fulfill God's determined purpose, which he planned before the foundation of the earth, to bring about the redemption of all things in Christ.

Edwards' insistence on God's redemptive purpose, planned in eternity, before the foundation of Creation is certainly not without biblical warrant. The scriptures,

---

32  Ibid., 7.

on several accounts, speak of God's purpose to plan the execution of redemption through his providential design. Ephesians 1:4, for example, explains, "even as he (The Father) chose us in him (Christ) before the foundation of the world, that we should be Holy and blameless before him." The Apostle Paul states, here, that God the Father is the author of redemption: he planned the choosing of his people in eternity, he purchased them in Christ for the purpose of making them Holy and blameless. The Father's determined purpose to bring about the redemption of the saints in Christ, through the execution of his providence, is apparent. The saints in Christ are presently being made holy and blameless and will be perfected in holiness and blamelessness because God the Father, in harmony with the Son and the Spirit, has ordained redemption before the foundations of the earth.

## 0.15 The Effects of Redemption

Edwards' writing conveys that redemption is one work that consists of different parts, or more accurately distinct dispensations (the Old Testament period, the Christ's incarnation, and the church age). Even though these dispensations had distinct characteristics, Edwards stresses that these individual dispensations were parts of the whole, which was the work of redemption in its entirety. Edwards observes:

> When it is said in the doctrine, that this is a work that God is carrying on from the fall of man to the end of the world, what I mean, is, that those things which belong

> to the work itself, and are parts of this scheme, are all this while accomplishing. There were some things done preparatory to its beginning, and the fruits of it will remain after it is finished. But the work itself was begun immediately upon the fall, and will continue to the end of the world, and then be finished: the various dispensations of God in this space belong to the same work, and to the same design, and have all one issue; and therefore are all to be reckoned but as several parts of one work, as it were, several successive motions of one machine, to bring about, in the conclusion one great event. [33]

Redemption, as Edwards observes, is 'one work,' which also consists of 'several parts.' The duration of time, extending from the fall of man to the end of the world, consisting of the successive dispensations, is the historical framework in which God has and will accomplish his redemptive purpose in keeping with his Word and Covenant promise. Edwards clearly identifies an eschatological outlook on redemptive history, from start to finish. God will, thereby, complete his work of redemption throughout the course of history, so that all things will conform to his design, planned in eternity past — the full disclosure of Christ's kingdom over creation.

In order to better understand God's accomplishment of the different parts of redemption, Edwards differentiates between 'the parts' of redemption. Edwards observes:

> We must distinguish between the parts of redemption itself, and the parts of that work by which redemption

---

33  Ibid., 9.

is wrought out. There is a difference between the parts
of the benefits procured and bestowed, and the parts
of that work of God by which those benefits were procured and bestowed. As for example, there is a difference
between the parts of the benefits that the children of
Israel received, in their redemption out of Egypt, and the
parts of that work of God by which this was wrought.
The redemption of the children of Israel out of Egypt,
considered as the benefit which they enjoyed, consisted
of two parts, namely, their deliverance from their former
Egyptian bondage and misery, and their being brought
into a more happy state, as the servants of God, and
heirs of Canaan.[34]

Edwards maintains that there is a categorical difference
between the parts of redemption, which are procured
and bestowed. To give a vivid example of the procurement of redemption and its bestowment, Edwards employs the biblical account of the Exodus. The Israelites
both enjoyed the release from the misery and bondage
imposed upon them by the Egyptians, but they also
enjoyed God's provision of Canaan as their inheritance. Deliverance from bondage was one dimension
of redemption, while God's bestowment of the land of
Canaan was another part — both, though, are equally
deemed as redemption. God was the agent of Israel's
deliverance from Egypt, and he was also the agent of
Israel's inheritance. One would be mistaken to mini-
mize the inheritance of Canaan as an aspect of redemption, while maintaining the redemptive deliverance

---

34  Ibid., 9.

from the Egyptian bondage, both parts of redemption are important in the grand design of God's redemptive purpose in Christ. Edwards, in understanding redemption in terms of procurement and bestowment wants his readers to recognize that God's work to deliver the church and creation from the curse is one act with different incremental parts.

Similarly, Edwards makes a clear distinction between the effects of redemption, relating to the souls of the redeemed and grand design in general. God's work of redemption, as it relates to the soul's deliverance from the captivity of sin, is not out of sync with God's grand design of redemption. Edwards observes that God has been actively involved in bringing about his redemptive purposes on an individual level. Commenting on the effects of redemption as it relates to the souls of the redeemed, Edwards states:

> With respect to the effect wrought on the souls of the redeemed, which is common to all ages. This effect is the application of redemption with respect to the souls of particular persons, in converting, justifying, sanctifying, and glorifying them. Thus sinners are actually redeemed; and receive the benefit of the work of redemption in its effect upon their souls. And in this sense the work of redemption is carried on from the fall of man.... The work of God in converting souls, opening blind eyes, unstopping deaf ears, raising the spiritually dead to life, and rescuing miserable captives out of the hands of Satan,

was begun soon after the fall of man, has been carried on ever since, and will be to the end.[35]

We see, from Edwards' observation, here, that the redemption of souls is the normative and continuous pattern that extends throughout redemptive history. God's purpose in justifying, sanctifying, and glorifying the church has and will remain a constant between the period of the fall and the end of the world.

Of course, the justification, sanctification, and glorification of souls is within the broader context of the grand design of redemption. Edwards writes the following on the effects of redemption as it relates to the grand design in general:

> The work of redemption with respect to the grand design in general, as it respects the universal subject and end, is carried on in a different manner, not merely be repeating or renewing the same effect in the different subjects of it, but *by many successive works and dispensation of God, all tending to one great end, all united as the several parts of one scheme, and all together making up one great work:* like as when a house or temple is being built; first the workmen are engaged, then the materials are collected, the ground prepared, the foundation laid, the superstructure erected, one part after another, till at length the top-stone is laid, and all finished. Now the work of redemption in that extensive sense which has been explained, may be compared to such a building. God began it immediately after the fall, as may be shown hereafter, and has proceeded, as it were, collecting materials, and building, ever since;

---

35  Ibid., 10.

and so… will continue to the end of the world; and then shall the top-stone be brought forth, and the whole appear complete and glorious.[36]

Edwards puts emphasis on the reality that, though there are many 'successive works' and 'dispensations,' which God purposed to be parts of the grand design of redemption, the course of redemption has one grand design. This means that the Exodus, the institution of the ceremonial laws, incarnation of Christ, and the justification, sanctification, and glorification of the church all have one and the same purpose, which is the design that God is providentially bringing about throughout the course of history, that which will finally be fulfilled at Christ's coming.

## 0.16 The Design of Redemption

The design of redemption, as Edwards describes it, focuses on the things, which "are intended to be accomplished by it".[37] Edwards, in the effort to help his read ers grasp what he means by the 'things…accomplished by redemption,' gives the illustration of a workman, what he is about, and the steps he pursues to accomplish a piece of work and what he intends to do with that work. If we fail to grasp what the work man is about, the steps that a workman pursues in building his craft, and his intention for that work, Edwards maintains that the casual observer will "see nothing of his scheme, and understand nothing of what he means by

---

36  Ibid., 11.
37  Ibid., 12.

it." Edwards goes on further to compare the design of redemption with the work of an architect by explaining:

> If an architect, with a great number of hands, were building some great palace, and one that was a stranger to such a thing should stand by, and see some men digging in the earth, others bringing timber, others hewing stones, and the like, he might see that there was a great deal done; but if he knew not the design, it would all appear to him as confusion. And therefore, that the great works and dispensations of God which belong to this great affair of redemption may not appear like confusion to you.[38]

The casual observer, according to Edwards, in having no insight into the what the architect is going about doing, the steps he pursues, or his overall intention, will appear confusing to him. He might delight in and admire the complex design and the beauty of that palace, while being, at the same time, unaware of the work put into the palace, and its intricate design. The unbeliever, similar to this casual observer, might be capable to read of the design of redemption in scripture, while being, at the same time, completely unaware of God's person, God's steps to bring about redemption, and its design. This begs the question: What is the design of redemption as Edwards understands it from the Word of God? Edwards, in *The History of Redemption*, describes five things the design of redemption accomplishes:

---

38  Ibid., 12.

- To put all of God's enemies under his feet;
- To perfectly restore the ruins of the fall;
- To gather together into one, all things in Christ;
- To glorify the whole church;
- To accomplish the glory of the Trinity in eminent degree.

## 0.17 To Put All of God's Enemies Under His Feet

The *Proto-Evangelion* in Gen 3:15 is the first scriptural instance where God declares the promise of the gospel. Interestingly, God's victory over his enemies through the seed of the woman is the emphasis of this promise: "I will put enmity between you and the woman, and between your offspring and her offspring; he shall bruise your head, and you shall bruise his heal." Now one would not be remiss to conclude from the *Proto-Evangelion* that one design of redemption is Christ's imperialistic conquest over the kingdom of Satan. Though Satan would temporarily inflict harm on the seed of the woman, the design of redemption would ultimately witness Christ's victory over the serpent. Edwards understood Christ's final victory over all his enemies as a central pillar to the design of redemption. Edwards observes:

> Now one grand design of God in the affair of redemption was, to reduce and subdue those of his enemies till they should all be out under his feet; 'He must reign till he hath put all his enemies under his feet,' I Cor. 15:25. Things were originally so planned, that he might disappoint, confound, and triumph over Satan, and that

he might be bruised under Christ's feet, Gen. 3:15. The promise was given, that the Seed of the woman should bruise the serpent's head. It was a part of God's original design in this work, to destroy the work of the devil, and confound him in all his purposes: 'For this purpose was the Son of God manifested, that he might destroy the works of the devil,' 1 John 3:8. It was a part of his design, to triumph over sin, and over the corruptions of men, and to root them out of the hearts of his people, by conforming them to himself. He designed also, that his grace should triumph over man's guilt, and the infinite demerit which is in sin. Again, it was a part of his design to triumph over death; and, however, this is the last enemy that shall be overcome, yet that shall finally be vanquished and destroyed.[39]

Christ will, in Edwards' view, subdue all of his enemies. Referencing the biblical foundation of 1 Cor 15:25, along with Gen 3:15 and 1 John 3:8, Edwards relishes in the hope that Christ will 'disappoint,' 'confound,' and ultimately 'triumph' over the kingdom of Satan. Edwards, here, undoubtedly upholds the notion that the design of redemption is an imperialistic enterprise on the part of the Triune God. Of course, Edwards, in highlighting Christ's triumphant victory over the kingdom of Satan, sees the conversion of men as a critical component to the victorious advancement of his eternal Kingdom. The disappointment, confoundment, and triumph of Christ over all his enemies would be realized as he manifests his grace in the hearts of his

---

39 Ibid., 13-14.

people, the church: Christ would, as a testimony to his perfect obedience as the perfect law-keeper and wrath-bearer, root out their sinful corruptions, conforming them to himself. But Christ's redemptive design to triumph over his enemies through conversion was not the final extent to which his victory would eventually be realized. The final realization of Christ's victory over his enemies, as Edwards observes, will finally come with his triumph over the last enemy, which is death. This last enemy will, as Edwards puts it, "shall finally be vanquished and destroyed."

## 0.18 To Perfectly Restore the Ruins of the Fall

The full restoration of creation in Christ is a central tenet the sets Christianity apart from all pagan worldviews. Christianity is, in fact, unique in the sense that all creation, being good in its essence, will be delivered and restored with the redeemed. The outcome of redemptive history is clearly cosmic in its scope. Edwards, in understanding the correlation between the redemption of the church and restoration of creation in its entirety, typically adhered to the confession that every aspect of the created order will be saved with the souls, ruined by the fall. Edwards writes:

> Man's soul was ruined by the fall; the image of God was defaced; man's nature was corrupted, and he became dead in sin. The design of God was, to restore the soul of man; to restore life, and the image of God, in conversion; and to carry on this work in sanctification, until he should perfect it in glory. Man's body was ruined; by the fall it

became subject to death. The design of God was to restore it from this ruin, and not only to deliver it from death, by the resurrection, but to deliver it from mortality itself, in making it like into Christ's glorious body. The world was ruined, as to man, as effectually as if it had been reduced to choose again; all heaven and earth were overthrown. But the design of God was, to restore all, and as it were to create a new heaven and a new earth.[40]

A comprehensive analysis of what Edwards is saying in this instance clearly highlights his insistence upon the Christian confession that the redemption of Christ is cosmic in its scope. Even though man's soul was brought to ruin by the fall, Edwards insists that God, in keeping with his overall design in redemption, will restore life in its totality in the Son, Jesus Christ. The sanctification of the redeemed in Christ, consequently, has universal ramifications, which cannot be ignored. The Trinity harmoniously established the created order, not only as the stage in which redemption would take place, but also as the dwelling place for man. If creation is good in its essence, then creation's restoration with the redemption of the church is a forgone conclusion. This is, at least, consistent with Edwards' outlook on the scope of redemption. The eschatological design of God's redemptive purpose is the restoration of life in harmony with the restoration of the *Imago Dei* (The Image of God) as God has, since the fall, carried on his work of sanctification until it's completion at the end of the world. Edwards, in having an optimistic outlook

---

40   Ibid., 14-15.

in his eschatology, clearly understood the new heavens and the new earth in terms of the restoration, not the destruction, of creation, which, of course, was in correlation with the sanctification of the church.

## 0.19 To Gather Together into One, All Things in Christ

The modern evangelical church, heavily influenced by pietism, reduces the effect of redemption to personal faith and individualized spirituality. Though the redemption does indeed impact the individual level, Christians, who are influenced by pietism, easily fall into the trap of reductionism in assuming that the impact of the gospel is *solely* relevant to evangelism, oversees missions, and personal conversions. Edwards, in contrast, in keeping with texts like Ephesians 1:7-10, confesses that the impact of redemption has a cosmic effect. Edwards writes:

> Another great design of God in the work of redemption was to gather together in one, all things in Christ, both in heaven and in earth, that is, all elect creatures in heaven and in earth, to a union, in one body, under one head: and to unite all together in one body to God the Father. This was begun soon after the fall, and is carried on throughout all ages, and shall be finished at the end of the world.[41]

Edwards clearly understands that the scope of redemption extends far beyond one's personal faith. The work of redemption, as Edwards puts it, is the gathering or perfect union of all things in creation under Jesus

---

41  Ibid., 15.

Christ. Redemption, for Edwards, is undoubtably a cosmic redemption. In fact, the union of all things in creation in Christ has been the grand design of redemption since the fall. Edwards, by asserting that the work of redemption began immediately after the fall and will be completed at the end of the world, cherishes an understanding of history that is Christological in every respect, which leads to the following conclusion: the work of creation, the fall, and the course of redemptive history exists to ultimately glorify Jesus at the end of the world. In Ephesians 1:7-10, the Apostle Paul says:

> In him we have redemption through his blood, the forgiveness of our trespasses, according to the riches of his grace, which he lavished upon us, in all wisdom and insight making known to us the mystery of his will, according to his purpose, which he set forth in Christ as a plan for the fullness of time, to unite all things in him, things in heaven and things on earth.

Here, we see that Edwards' understanding of redemption is quite consistent with the Apostle Paul's understanding. Because Christian believers are redeemed by the blood of Christ, God makes the mystery of his will known to them, which is the cosmic design of redemption, the union of all things in heaven and earth in Christ. Edwards, therefore, in keeping with the biblical witness, ascribes to a cosmic understanding of redemption, which glorifies the prominence of Jesus Christ over all things. For Edwards, the glorification of Christ is the chief end of the work of redemption.

## 0.20 To Glorify the Whole Church

Edwards cherished a high view of the church precisely because Christ himself cherishes a high view of his church. God will, according to Edwards, complete the glory of the elect as an additional component to the design of redemption. Edwards writes:

> God designs by this work to perfect and complete the glory of all the elect of Christ. To advance them to an exceeding pitch of glory, 'such as eye hath not seen, nor ear heard, nor has ever entered into the heart of man.' He intends to bring them to perfect excellency and beauty in his image, and in holiness, which is the proper beauty of spiritual beings; and to advance them to a glorious degree of honour, an ineffable height of pleasure and joy, and thus to glorify the whole church of elect men in soul and body; and with them to bring the glory of the elect angels to its highest elevation under one head.[42]

Edwards links the beauty and the excellence of the elect with holiness. In fact, the true excellence and beauty of the whole person is inseparable from holiness. The church's elevation to such a state of glorious beauty is rooted in the holiness of the church's one head, Jesus Christ. Edwards draws his readers to ponder the intricate relationship between holy excellence and the beauty of Christ and that of the elect. The church is, thereby, glorified with Christ, since the people of God are in Christ. The weight of such anticipated glory gives Christian believers reason to delight in the excellence and beauty that comes with holiness, even in a

---

42  Ibid., 15-16.

fallen state, because of the anticipated certainty of 'the height of pleasure' in true excellence and true beauty that will come with the eternal fellowship. Edwards' writing shows his unyielding confidence and comfort in the reality that Christ will fully glorify his church at the appointed time.

## 0.21 To Accomplish the Glory of the Trinity in Eminent Degree

The modern church, over the last fifty years, has placed a great deal of undue attention on personal salvation, as though the conversion of sinners is the key priority of God's redemptive design, and as though the good of man is the focal point of God's redemptive purpose. Such an outlook on this modern conclusion of redemption would be foreign and even distressing to Edwards. Though Edwards would certainly not deny the importance of personal conversion as one piece of the grand fabric of redemption, he would, nonetheless, insist that the glory of God is the chief purpose of redemptive history. Personal salvation, thereby, has a greater purpose than the personal joy that comes with being found in Christ. For Edwards, the glory of God is the great purpose of redemption's design. In fact, in Edwards' view, the subduing of Christ's enemies, creation's restoration from the ruins of the fall, the gathering of all things in Christ, and the glorification of the whole church cannot stand on their own, apart from God's chief purpose to glorify his own name in the work and design of redemption. Edwards writes:

God had a design from eternity to glorify each person in the Godhead. The end must be considered as first in order of nature, and then the means; and therefore we must conceive, that God having professed this end, had then, as it were, the means to choose; and the principal mean that he pitched upon was this great work of redemption which we are speaking of. It was his design in this work to glorify his only begotten Son, Jesus Christ; and by the Son to glorify the Father: 'Now is the Son of man glorified in him, and God is glorified in him. If God be glorified in him, God also shall glorify him in himself, and shall straightway glorify him,' John 13:31-32. It was his design that the Son should thus be glorified, and should glorify the Father by what should be accomplished by the Spirit, to the glory of the Spirit; that the whole Trinity conjunctly, and each person distinctly, might be exceedingly glorified.[43]

Edwards observes the harmonious design of the Godhead, planned in eternity, to bring glory to each member of the Trinity through redemption. Readers of Edwards will notice his understanding of the way in which God has ordained to exalt his glory, namely through the mutual harmony that existed among each member of the Trinity in eternity. Edwards mentions the design of the Son and the Father to mutually glorify each other through redemption. The Son, by the perfection of his obedience, sought to honour the Father as the chief object of his mission while on earth. In fact, Christ's chief delight in his ministry was to give due honour to

---

43  Ibid., 16.

his Father. The Father, in turn, manifested his delight in the Son, publicly making known the glory of Christ, while the Holy Spirit brings glory to the Father and the Son through the advancement of the Kingdom of God, accomplished through the regeneration of God's people. Edwards' assertion is that Christ is the chief reason for creation's existence. God's purpose to honour his name, through the mutual harmony of the Trinity, is the first priority of the natural world. The philosophical implication of God's chief purpose to honour his name is that everything in the created realm was created for the purpose of honouring each member of the Trinity in the grand narrative of redemptive history.

## 0.22 Conclusion

In conclusion, Edwards would indeed depart from the modern portrayal of Jesus by insisting that the incarnation of Jesus was one part (as important as that might be) of the grander design of redemptive history. Furthermore, by application, Christ is the exclusive and primary agent, who has worked on behalf of his church, since the fall. Edwards' writing highlights that redemptive history has one Christological design, consisting of three parts, the preparation of Christ's coming, Christ's purchase, and, finally, the age of the Spirit, where Christ extends his Kingdom through the gathering of his church. Edwards' doctrinal understanding of redemption hinges on Isaiah 51:8, which is a reminder to us that the Triune God is the great comforter of his church, bringing to mind his promised salvation, and with this, the deliverance from her enemies.

Edwards points out that the church's inheritance, and her happy state in Christ, unlike that of her enemies, is guarded because of his righteousness. In explaining this, Edwards identifies the relationship between God's righteousness and his salvation: God remains faithful to his promise of salvation because of his righteousness. Edwards, consequently, sees the timeframe for purchasing the church from the grips of sin as taking place over the *entire* course of history. The design of redemption, as Edwards explains, are the things "intended to be accomplished by it;" putting all of God's enemies under his feet, perfectly restoring the ruins of the fall, gathering together into one, all things in Christ, glorifying the whole church, and finally, accomplishing the glory of the Trinity in eminent degree. Edwards' confessional understanding of redemptive history, therefore, bids the modern church to cherish God's universal design to bring all things under the dominion of Jesus Christ, the church's advocate and mediator.

*Soli Deo Gloria*

# The History of Redemption
# Period I - From the Fall to the Incarnation

*Jonathan Edwards*

## 1.0 Introductory Words

THE GREAT WORKS OF GOD in the world during this whole space of time were all preparatory to this. There were many great changes and revolutions in the world, but they were all only the turning of the wheels of providence to make way for the coming of Christ and what he was to do in the world. Hither tended especially all God's great works towards his church. The church was under varioius dispensations of providence, and in various circumstances, before Christ came; but all these dispensations were to prepare the way for his coming. God wrought salvation for the souls of men through all that space of time, though the number was very small to what it was afterwards; and all this was by way of anticipation. All the souls that were saved before Christ came, were only the earnests of the future harvest.

God wrought many deliverances for his church and people before Christ came; but these were only images and forerunners of the great salvation. The church during that space of time enjoyed the light of divine revelation. They had in a degree the light of the gospel. But all these revelations were only so many earnests of the great light that he should bring who came to be the light of the world. That whole space of time was the time of night, wherein the church of God was not indeed wholly without light; but it was like the light of the moon and stars; a dim light in comparison of the light of the sun, and mixed with a great deal of darkness. It had no glory by reason of the glory that excelleth, 2 Cor. 3:10. The church had indeed the light of the sun, but it was only as reflected from the moon and stars. The church all that while was a minor. Gal. 4:1-3,

> Now I say, that the heir as long as he is a child, differeth nothing from a servant, though he be lord of all; but is under tutors and governors, until the time appointed of the Father. Even so we, when we were children, were in bondage under the elements of the world.

But here, for the greater clearness and distinctness, shall subdivide this period into parts:

1ST, From the fall to the flood.
2D, From thence to the calling of Abraham.
3D, From thence to Moses.
4TH, From thence to David.
5TH, From David to the captivity in Babylon.
6TH, From thence to the incarnation of Christ.

## 1.1 PART I
### From the Fall to the Flood

THOUGH THIS PERIOD was the most distant from Christ's incarnation; yet then was this glorious building begun.

**I.** As soon as man fell, Christ entered on his mediatorial work. Then it was that he began to execute the work and office of a mediator. He had undertaken it before the world was made. He stood engaged with the Father to appear as man's mediator, and to take on that office when there should be occasion, from all eternity. But now the time was come. Christ the eternal Son of God clothed himself with the mediatorial character, and therein presented himself before the Father. He immediately stepped in between a holy, infinite, offended Majesty, and offending mankind. He was accepted in his interposition; and so wrath was prevented from going forth in the full execution of that amazing curse that man had brought on himself.

It is manifest that Christ began to exercise the office of mediator between God and man as soon as every man fell, because mercy began to be exercised towards man immediately.

There was mercy in the forbearance of God, that he did not destroy him, as he did the angels when they fell. But there is no mercy exercised toward fallen man but through a mediator. If God had not in mercy restrained Satan, he would immediately have seized on his prey. Christ began to do the part of an intercessor for man as soon as man fell; for there is no mercy exercised towards man but what is obtained through Christ's intercession. From that day Christ took on him the care of the church, in the exercise of all his offices. He undertook to teach mankind in the exercise of his prophetical office; to intercede for fallen man in his priestly office; and to govern the church and the world as a king. He from that time took upon him the care of defending his elect church from all their enemies. When Satan, the grand enemy, had conquered and overthrown man, the business of resisting and conquering him was committed to Christ. He thenceforward undertook to manage that subtle powerful adversary. He was then appointed the Captain of the Lord's hosts, the Captain of their salvation. Henceforward this lower world, with all its concerns, devolved upon the Son of God: for when man had sinned, God the Father would have no more to do immediately with this world of mankind, that had apostatized from and rebelled against him. He would henceforward act only through a mediator, either in teaching men, or in governing, or bestowing any benefits on them.

And therefore, when we read in sacred history what God did, from time to time, towards his church and people, and how he revealed himself to them, we are to understand it especially of the second person of the Trinity. When we read of God appearing after the fall, in some visible form or outward symbol of his presence, we are ordinarily, if not universally, to understand it of the second person of the Trinity. John 1:18, "No man hath seen God at any time; the only begotten Son, which is in the bosom of the Father, he hath declared him." He is therefore called "the image of the invisible God," Col. 1:15, intimating, that though God the Father be invisible, yet Christ is his image or representation, by which he is seen.

Yea, not only this lower world devolved on Christ, that he might have the care and government of it, and order it agreeably to his design of redemption, but also in some respect the whole universe. The angels from that time are subject to him in his mediatorial office, as is manifest by the scripture history, wherein we have accounts of their acting as ministering spirits in the affairs of the church.

And therefore, we may suppose, that immediately on the fall of Adam, it was made known in heaven among the angels, that God had a design of redemption with respect to fallen man; that Christ had now taken upon him the office and work of a mediator between God and man; and that they were to be subservient to him in this office. And as Christ, in this office, has been solemnly installed the King of heaven, and is thenceforward, as God-man, the Light, the Sun of heaven, (agreeable to Rev. 21:23.) so this revelation made in heaven among the angels, was as it were the first dawning of this light there. When Christ ascended into heaven after his passion, and was solemnly enthroned, then this Sun rose in heaven, even the Lamb that is the light of the New Jerusalem.

**II.** Presently upon this the gospel was first revealed on earth, in these words, Gen. 3:15,

> And I will put enmity between thee and the woman, and
> between thy seed and her seed: it shall bruise thy head,
> and thou shalt bruise his heel.

We must suppose, that God's intention of redeeming fallen man was first signified in heaven, before it was signified on earth, because the business of the angels as ministering spirits of the Mediator required it; for as soon as ever Christ had taken on him the work of a mediator, it was requisite that the angels should be ready immediately to be subservient to him in that office: so that the light first dawned in heaven; but very soon after the same was signified on earth. In those words of God there was an intimation of another surety to be appointed for man, after the first surety had failed. This was the first revelation of the covenant of grace; the first dawning of the light of the gospel on earth.

This lower world before the fall enjoyed noon-day light; the light of the knowledge of God, the light of his glory, and the light of his favour. But when man fell, all this light was at once extinguished, and the world reduced back again to total darkness; a worse darkness than that which was in the beginning of the world (Gen. 1:2). Darkness was upon the face of the deep, a darkness a thousand times more remediless than that. Neither men nor angels could find out any way whereby this darkness might be scattered. It appeared in its blackness when Adam and his wife saw that they were naked, and sewed fig-leaves; when they heard the voice of the Lord

God, walking in the garden, and hid themselves among the trees. When God first called them to an account, and said to Adam, "What is this that thou hast done? Hast thou eaten of the tree, whereof I commanded thee, that thou shouldst not eat?" Then we may suppose that their hearts were filled with shame and terror. But these words of God (Gen. 3:15) were the first dawning of gospel light, after this dismal darkness. Before this there was not one glimpse of light, any beam of comfort, or the least hope. It was an obscure yet comprehensive revelation of the gospel; not indeed made to Adam or Eve directly, but contained in what God said to the serpent.

Here was a certain intimation of a merciful design by "the seed of the woman," which was like the first glimmerings of the light in the east when the day first dawns. This intimation of mercy was given, even before sentence was pronounced on either Adam or Eve, from tenderness to them, lest they should be overborne with a sentence of condemnation, without having anything held forth whence they could gather any hope.

One of those great things that were intended to be done by the work of redemption, is more plainly intimated, viz. God subduing his enemies under the feet of his Son. God's design of this was now first declared. Satan probably had triumphed greatly in the fall of man, as though he had defeated the designs of God in his creation. But in these words, God gives him a plain intimation, that he should not finally triumph, but that a complete victory and triumph should be obtained over him by the seed of the woman.

This revelation of the gospel was the first thing that Christ did in his prophetical office. From the fall of man to the incarnation of Christ, God was doing those things that were preparatory to Christ's coming to effect redemption, and were forerunners and earnests of it. And one of those things was to foretell and promise it, as he did from age to age, till Christ came. This was the first promise given, the first prediction that ever was made of it.

**III.** Soon after this, the custom of sacrificing was appointed, to be a standing type of the sacrifice of Christ, till he should come, and offer up himself a sacrifice to God. Sacrificing was not a custom first established by the Levitical law, for it had been a part of God's instituted worship from the beginning. We read of the patriarchs, Abraham, Isaac, and Jacob, offering sacrifice, and before them Noah, and Abel. And this was by divine appointment; for it was part of God's worship in his church, which was offered up in faith, and which he accepted. This proves that it was by his institution; for sacrificing is no part of natural worship. The light of nature doth not teach men to offer up beasts in sacrifice to God; and seeing it was not enjoined by the law of nature, to be acceptable to God, it must be by some positive command or institution; for God has declared his abhorrence of such worship as is taught by the precept of men without his institution (Isa. 29:13). And such worship as hath not a warrant from divine institution, cannot be offered up in faith, because faith has no foundation where there is no divine appointment.

Men have no warrant to hope for God's acceptance, in that which is not of his appointment, and in that to which he hath not promised his acceptance: and therefore, it follows, that the custom of offering sacrifices to God was instituted soon after the fall; for the Scripture teaches us, that Abel offered "the firstlings of his flock, and of the fat thereof," Gen. 4:4, and that he was accepted of God in this offering, Heb. 11:4. And there is nothing in the story intimating that the institution was first given when Abel offered up that sacrifice to God; but rather that Abel only complied with a custom already established.

It is very probable that sacrifice was instituted immediately after God had revealed the covenant of grace, (Gen. 3:15.) as the foundation on which the custom of sacrificing was built. That promise was the first stone laid towards this glorious building, the work of redemption; and the next stone, the institution of sacrifices, to be a type of the great sacrifice.

The next thing that we have an account of, after God had pronounced sentence on the serpent, on the woman, and on the man, was, that God made them coats of skins, and clothed them; which, by the generality of divines, are thought to be the skins of beasts slain in sacrifice. For we have no account of anything else that should be the occasion of man's slaying beasts, except to offer them in sacrifice, till after the flood. Men were not wont to eat the flesh of beasts as their common food till after the flood. The first food of man before the fall, was the fruit of the trees of paradise; and after the fall, his food was the produce of the field: Gen. 3:18, "And thou shalt eat the herb of the field." The first grant that he had to eat flesh, as his common food, was after the flood: Gen. 9:3, "Every moving thing that liveth shall be meat for you; even as the green herb have I given you all things." So that it is likely that these skins with which Adam and Eve were clothed, were the skins of their sacrifices. God's clothing them with these was a lively figure of their being clothed with the righteousness of Christ. It was God that gave them this clothing; for it is said, God made them coats of skins, and clothed them. The righteousness with which we are clothed, is of God. It is he only that clothes the naked soul.

Our first parents, who were naked, were clothed at the expense of life. Beasts were slain, in order to afford them clothing. So doth Christ, to afford clothing to our naked souls. The tabernacle in the wilderness, which signified the church, was covered with rams' skins died red, as though they were dipped in blood, to signify that Christ's righteousness was wrought out through the pains of death, under which he shed his precious blood.

We observed before, that the light that the church enjoyed from the fall of man, till Christ came, was like the light which we enjoy in the night; not the light of the sun directly, but as reflected from the moon and other luminaries; which light prefigured Christ, the Sun of righteousness that was afterwards to arise. This light they had chiefly two ways; one was by predictions of Christ to come; the other was by types and shadows, whereby his coming and redemption were prefigured. The first thing that was done to prepare the way for Christ in the former of these ways, was in that promise noticed in the foregoing particular; and the first thing of the latter kind, was that institution of sacrifices that we are now upon. As that promise in Gen. 3:15 was the first dawn of gospel-light after the fall in prophecy; so the institution of sacrifices was the first hint of it in types. The former was done in pursuance of Christ's prophetical office; in the latter, Christ exhibited himself in his priestly office.

The institution of sacrifices was a great thing done towards preparing the way for Christ's coming and working out redemption. For the sacrifices of the Old Testament were the main of all the Old-Testament types of Christ and his redemption; and it tended to establish in the minds of God's visible church the necessity of a propitiatory sacrifice, in order to the Deity's being satisfied for sin; and so prepared the way for the reception of the glorious gospel, that reveals the great sacrifice in the visible church, and not only so, but through the world of mankind. For from this institution of sacrifices all nations derived the custom of sacrificing to the gods, to atone for their sins. No nation, however barbarous, was found without it. This is a great evidence of the truth of the Christian religion; for no nation except the Jews, could tell how they came by this custom, or to what purpose it was to offer sacrifices to their deities. The light of nature did not teach them any such thing. That did not teach them that the gods were hungry, and fed upon the flesh which they burnt in sacrifice; and yet they all had this custom; of which no other account can be given, but that they derived it from Noah, who had it from his ancestors, on whom God had enjoined it as a type of the great sacrifice of Christ. However, by this means all nations of the world had their minds possessed with this notion, that an atonement or sacrifice for sin was necessary; and a way was made for their more readily receiving the great doctrine of the gospel, the atonement and sacrifice of Christ.

**IV.** God soon after the fall began actually to save the souls of men through Christ's redemption. In this, Christ, who had lately taken upon him the work of mediator between God and man, did first begin that work, wherein he appeared in the exercise of his kingly office, as in the sacrifices he was represented in his priestly office, and in the first prediction of redemption by Christ he had appeared in the exercise of his prophetical office. In that prediction the light of Christ's redemption first began to dawn in the prophecies of it; in the institution of sacrifices it first began to dawn in the types of it; in this, viz. his beginning actually to save men, it first began to dawn in the fruit of it.

It is probable, therefore, that Adam and Eve were the first fruits of Christ's redemption; it is probable by God's manner of treating them, by his comforting them as he did, after their awakenings and terror. They were awakened, and ashamed with a sense of their guilt, after their eyes were opened, and they saw that they were naked, and sewed fig-leaves to cover their nakedness; as the sinner, under the first awakenings, is wont to endeavour to hide the nakedness of his soul, by a fancied righteousness of his own. Then they were further terrified and awakened, by hearing the voice of God as he was coming to condemn them. Their coverings of fig-leaves do not answer the purpose; but notwithstanding these, they ran to hide themselves among the trees of the garden, because they were naked, not daring to trust to their fig-leaves to hide their nakedness from God. Then they were further awakened by God's calling of them to a strict account. But while their terrors were raised to such a height, and they stood, as we may suppose, trembling and astonished before their Judge, without any expedient whence they could gather any hope, then God took care to hold forth some encouragement, to keep them from the dreadful effects of despair under their awakenings, by giving a hint of a design of mercy by a Saviour, even before he pronounced sentence against them. And when after this he proceeded to pronounce sentence, whereby we may suppose their terrors were further raised, God soon after took care to encourage them, and to let them see, that he had not wholly cast them off, by taking a fatherly care of them in their fallen, naked, and miserable state, by making them coats of skins and clothing them. Which also manifested an acceptance of those sacrifices that they offered to God, which were types of what God had promised, when he said, "The seed of the woman shall bruise the serpent's head." This promise, there is reason to think, they believed and embraced. Eve seems plainly to express her hope in and dependence on that promise, in what she says at the birth of Cain, Gen.

4:1, "I have gotten a man from the Lord;" i.e. as God has promised, that my seed should bruise the serpent's head; so now has God given me this pledge and token of it, and I have a seed born. She plainly owns, that this child was from God, and hoped that her promised seed was to be of this, her eldest son; though she was mistaken, as Abraham was with respect to Ishmael, as Isaac was with respect to Esau, and as Samuel was with respect to the first-born of Jesse. And especially does what she said at the birth of Seth, express her hope and dependence on the promise of God; Gen. 4:25, "For God hath appointed me another seed, instead of Abel, whom Cain slew."

Thus it is exceeding probable, if not evident, that as Christ took on him the work of mediator as soon as man fell; so that he now immediately began his work of redemption in its effect, and that he immediately encountered his great enemy the devil, whom he had undertaken to conquer, and rescued those two first captives out of his hands; therein baffling him, soon after his triumph over them, whereby he had made them his captives. And though he seemed sure of them and all their posterity, Christ the Redeemer soon showed him, that he was mistaken. He let him see it, in delivering those first captives, and so soon gave him an instance of the fulfilment of that threatening, "The seed of the woman shall bruise the serpent's head"; and in this instance a presage of his subduing all his enemies under his feet.

After this we have another instance of redemption in one of their children, righteous Abel, as the Scripture calls him; whose soul perhaps was the first that went to heaven through Christ's redemption. In him we have at least the first recorded instance of the death of a redeemed person. If he was the first, then as the redemption of Christ began to dawn before in the souls of men in their conversion and justification, in him it first began to dawn in glorification; and in him the angels began first to do the part of ministering spirits to Christ, in going forth to conduct to glory the souls of the redeemed. And in him the elect angels in heaven had the first opportunity to see so wonderful a thing as the soul of one of the fallen race of mankind, that had been sunk by the fall into such an abyss of sin and misery, brought to heaven, and in the enjoyment of heavenly glory, which was a much greater thing than if they had seen him returned to the earthly paradise. Thus they saw the glorious effect of Christ's redemption, in the great honour and happiness that was procured for sinful, miserable creatures.

V. The next remarkable thing that God did in further carrying on this great redemption, was the first uncommon pouring out of the Spirit, through Christ, in the days of Enos. We read, Gen. 4:26, "Then began men to call upon the name of the Lord." The meaning of those words has been considerably controverted among divines. We cannot suppose the meaning is, that then first men performed the duty of prayer. Prayer is a duty of natural religion, and a duty to which a spirit of piety does most naturally lead men. Prayer is the very breath of a spirit of piety; we cannot suppose, therefore, that holy men before, for above two hundred years, had lived without prayer. Therefore, some divines think, that the meaning is, that then men first began to perform public worship, or to call upon the name of the Lord in public assemblies. However, thus much must necessarily be understood by it, viz. that there was something new in the visible church of God with respect to calling upon the name of the Lord; that there was a great addition to the performance of this duty; and that in some respect or other it was carried far beyond what it ever had been before, which must be the consequence of a remarkable pouring out of the Spirit of God.

If it was now first that men were stirred up to meet in assemblies to assist one another in seeking God, so as they never had done before; it argues something extraordinary as the cause, and could be from nothing but the uncommon influences of God's Spirit. We see by experience, that a remarkable pouring out of God's Spirit is always attended with such an effect, viz. a great increase of the performance of the duty of prayer. When the Spirit of God begins a work on men's hearts, it immediately sets them to calling on the name of the Lord. As it was with Paul after the Spirit of God had arrested him; Behold, he prayeth! so it has been in all remarkable effusions of the Spirit of God recorded in Scripture; and so it is foretold it will be in the latter days. It is foretold, that the Holy Spirit will be poured out as a spirit of grace and supplication, Zech. 11:10. See also Zeph. 3:9, "For then will I turn to the people a pure language, that they may all call upon the name of the Lord, to serve him with one consent."

And when it is said, "Then began men to call upon the name of the Lord," no more can be intended by it, than that this was the first remarkable season of this nature that ever was. It was the beginning, or the first, of such a work of God. In this manner such an expression is commonly used in Scripture: so, 1 Sam. 14:35, "And Saul built an altar unto the Lord; the same was the first altar that he built unto the Lord." In the Hebrew it is, as you may see in the margin, that altar he began to build unto the Lord. Heb. 2:3, "How shall we escape if we neglect so great salvation, which first began to be spoken by the Lord?"

It may here be observed, that from the fall of man, to our day, the work of redemption in its effect has mainly been carried on by remarkable communications of the Spirit of God. Though there be a more constant influence of God's Spirit always in some degree attending his ordinances; yet the way in which the greatest things have been done towards carrying on this work, always have been by remarkable effusions, at special seasons of mercy, as may fully appear hereafter in our further prosecution of our subject. And this in the days of Enos, was the first remarkable pouring out of the Spirit of God that ever was. There had been a saving work of God on the hearts of some before; but now God was pleased to bring in a harvest of souls to Christ; so that in this we see that great building, of which God laid the foundation immediately after the fall of man, carried on further, and built higher, than ever it had been before.

**VI.** The next thing I shall notice, is the eminently holy life of Enoch, who, we have reason to think, was a saint of greater eminency than any that had been before him; so that in this respect the work of redemption was carried on to a still greater height. With respect to its effect in the visible church in general, we observed above how it was carried higher in the days of Enos than ever it had been before. Probably Enoch was one of the saints of that harvest; for he lived all the days that he did live on earth, in the days of Enos. And with respect to the degree to which this work was carried in the soul of a particular person, it was raised to a greater height in Enoch than ever before. His soul, built on Christ, was built up in holiness to a greater height than any preceding instance. He was a wonderful instance of Christ's redemption, and of the efficacy of his grace.

**VII.** In Enoch's time, God more expressly revealed the coming of Christ than he had before done. Jude 14, 15. "And Enoch also, the seventh from Adam, prophesied of these, saying, Behold, the Lord cometh with ten thousand of his saints, to execute judgment upon all, and to convince all that are ungodly among them, of their ungodly deeds which they have ungodly committed, and of all their hard speeches which ungodly sinners have spoken against him." Here Enoch prophesies of the coming of Christ. It does not seem to be confined to any particular coming of Christ; but it has respect in general to Christ's coming in his kingdom, and is fulfilled in a degree in both his first and second coming; and indeed, in every remarkable manifestation Christ has made of himself in the world, for the saving of his people, and the destroying of his enemies. It is very parallel in this respect with many other prophecies of the Old Testament; and, in particular, with that great prophecy of Christ's coming in his kingdom, whence the Jews principally took their notion of the kingdom of heaven. Daniel 7:10, "A fiery stream issued, and came forth from before him: thousand thousands ministered unto him, and ten thousand times ten thousand stood before him: the judgment was set, and the books were opened." And in Daniel 7:13, 14,

> I saw in the night visions, and behold, one like the Son of man, came with the clouds of heaven, and came to the Ancient of days, and they brought him near before him. And there was given him dominion, and glory, and a kingdom, that all people, nations, and languages, should serve him: his dominion is an everlasting dominion, which shall not pass away, and his kingdom that which shall not be destroyed.

And though it is not unlikely that Enoch might have a more immediate respect in this prophecy to the approaching destruction of the old world by the flood, which was a remarkable resemblance of Christ's destruction of all his enemies at his second coming, yet it doubtless looked beyond the type to the antitype.

And as this prophecy of Christ's coming is more express than any preceding it; so it is an instance of the increase of that gospel-light which began to dawn presently after the fall of man; and of that building which is the subject of our present discourse, being yet further carried on, and built up higher than it had been before.

And here, by the way, I would observe, that the increase of gospel-light, and the progress of the work of redemption, as it respects the church in general, from its erection to the end of the world, is very similar to the progress of the same word and the same light, in a particular soul, from the time of its conversion, till it is perfected and crowned in glory. Sometimes the light shines brighter, and at other times more obscurely; sometimes grace prevails, at other times it seems to languish for a great while together; now corruption prevails, and then grace revives again. But in general grace is growing: from its first infusion, till it is perfected in glory, the kingdom of Christ is building up in the soul. So it is with respect to the great affair in general, as it relates to the universal subject of it, and as it is carried on from its first beginning, till it is perfected at the end of the world.

**VIII.** The next remarkable thing towards carrying on this work, was the translation of Enoch into heaven. Gen. 5:24, "And Enoch walked with God, and he was not; for God took him." Moses, in giving an account of the genealogy of those that were of the line of Noah, does not say concerning Enoch, he lived so long and he died, as he does of the rest; but, he was not, for God took him; i.e. he translated him; in body and soul carried him to heaven without dying, as it is explained in Heb. 11:5, "By faith Enoch was translated that he should not see death." By this wonderful work of God, the work of redemption was carried to a greater height, in several respects, than it had been before.

When showing what God aimed at in the work of redemption, or what were the main things he intended to bring to pass; among other things I mentioned the perfect restoration of the ruins of the fall, with respect to the elect, both in soul and body. Now this translation of Enoch was the first instance of restoration with respect to the body. There had been many instances of restoring the soul of man by Christ's redemption, but none of redeeming and actually saving the body, till now. All the bodies of the elect are to be saved as well as their souls. At the end of the world, all their bodies shall actually be redeemed; those that then shall have been dead, by a resurrection; and others, that then shall be living, by causing them to undergo a glorious change. There was a number of the bodies of saints raised and glorified, at the resurrection of Christ; and before that there was an instance of a body glorified in Elijah. But the first instance of all was this of Enoch.

By this, the work of redemption was carried on still further; as, this wonderful work of God afforded a great increase of gospel-light to the church, hereby it had a clearer manifestation of a future state, and of the glorious reward of the saints in heaven. We are told, 2 Tim. 1:10, "That life and immortality are brought to light by the gospel." What was said in the Old Testament of a future state, is very obscure, in comparison with the more full, plain, and abundant revelation given of it in the New. But yet even in those early days, the church of God, in this instance, was favoured with an instance of it set before their eyes, in that one of their brethren was actually taken up to heaven without dying; which we have all reason to think the church of God knew then, as they afterwards knew Elijah's translation. And as this was a clearer manifestation of a future state than the church had enjoyed before, so it was a pledge or earnest of that future glorification of all the saints which God intended through the redemption of Jesus Christ.

**IX.** The next thing that I shall observe, was the upholding of the church of God in that family from which Christ was to proceed during that great and general defection which preceded the flood. The church of God, in all probability, was small, in comparison with the rest of the world, from the time that mankind began to multiply; or from the time, Gen. 4:16, "When Cain went out from the presence of the Lord, and dwelt in the land of Nod;" which being interpreted, is the land of banishment. The church seems to have been kept up chiefly in the posterity of Seth: for this was the seed that God appointed instead of Abel whom Cain slew. But we cannot reasonably suppose that Seth's posterity was one fiftieth part of the world: "For Adam was one hundred and thirty years old when Seth was born." But Cain, who seems to have been the leader of those that were not of the church, was Adam's eldest child, and probably was born soon after the fall, which doubtless was soon after Adam's creation; so that there was time for Cain to have many sons before Seth was born; besides many other children, that probably Adam and Eve had before this time, agreeably to God's blessing, "Be fruitful, and multiply, and replenish the earth;" and many of these children might have children. The history of Cain before Seth was born, seems to imply, that there were great numbers of men on the earth: Gen. 4:14-15,

> Behold, thou hast driven me out this day from the face of the earth: and from thy face shall I be hid, and I shall be a fugitive and a vagabond in the earth; and it shall come to pass, that every one that findeth me shall slay me. And the Lord said unto him, Therefore whosoever slayeth Cain, vengeance shall be taken on him seven-fold. And the Lord set a mark upon Cain, lest any finding him should kill him.

And all who existed when Seth was born, must be supposed to stand in equal capacity of multiplying their posterity with him; and therefore, Seth's posterity was but a small part of the inhabitants of the world.

But after the days of Enos and Enoch, (for Enoch was translated before Enos died,) the church of God greatly diminished, in proportion as multitudes of the line of Seth, born in the church of God, fell away, and joined with the wicked world, principally by means of intermarriages with them: as Gen. 4:1-2, 4,

> And it came to pass, when men began to multiply on the face of the earth, and daughters were born unto them, that the sons of God saw the daughters of men, that they

were fair; and they took them wives of all which they chose.—There were giants in the earth in those days; and also after that, when the sons of God came in unto the daughters of men, and they bare children to them, the same became mighty men, which were of old men of renown.

By the sons of God here, are doubtless meant the children of the church. It is a denomination often given them in Scripture. They intermarried with the wicked world, and so had their hearts led away from God: and there was a great and continual defection from the church. The church, that used to be a restraint on the wicked world, diminished exceedingly, and so wickedness went on without restraint. Satan, that old serpent the devil, that tempted our first parents, and set up himself as the God of this world, raged exceedingly; and every imagination of the thoughts of man's heart was only evil continually, and the earth was filled with violence. It seemed to be deluged with wickedness then, as it was with water afterwards; and mankind in general were swallowed up in it. And now Satan made a most violent and potent attempt to devour the church of God; and had almost done it. But yet God restored it in the midst of all this flood of wickedness and violence. He kept it up in that line of which Christ was to proceed. He would not suffer it to be destroyed, for a blessing was in it. There was a particular family, a root whence the branch of righteousness was afterwards to shoot forth. And therefore, however the branches were lopped off, and the tree seemed to be destroyed;

yet God, in the midst of all, kept alive this root, by his wonderful redeeming power and grace, so that the gates of hell could not prevail against it.

Thus, I have shown how God carried on the great affair of redemption; how the building went on during this first period, from the fall of man, till God brought the flood on the earth. And I would observe, that though the Mosaic history during that space be very short, yet it is exceedingly comprehensive and instructive. And it may also be profitable for us here to observe, the efficacy of that purchase of redemption which had such great effects so many ages before Christ actually appeared.

## 1.2 PART II
### 3.0 From the Flood to the Calling of Abraham

I PROCEED NOW to show how the same work was carried on from the beginning of the flood till the calling of Abraham. For though that mighty, universal deluge overthrew the world: yet it did not overthrow this building of God, the work of redemption. This went on; and instead of being overthrown, continued to be built up, in order to a further preparation for the great Saviour's coming into the world, for the redemption of his people.

**I.** The flood itself was a work of God that belonged to this great affair, and tended to promote it. All the mighty works of God from the fall of man to the end of the world, are reducible to this work; and if seen in a right view, will appear as parts of it; and so many steps for carrying it on; and doubtless so great a work, so remarkable and universal a catastrophe, as the deluge was, cannot be excepted. Thereby God removed out of the way the enemies and obstacles that were ready to overthrow it.

Satan seems to have been in a dreadful rage just before the flood, and his rage then doubtless was, as it always has been, chiefly against the church of God to overthrow it; and he had filled the earth with violence and rage against it. He had drawn over almost all the world to be on his side, and they listed under his banner against Christ and his church. We read, that the earth was filled with violence; and doubtless that violence was chiefly against the church, in fulfilment of what was foretold, "I will put enmity between thy seed and her seed." Their enmity and violence was so great, and the enemies of the church so numerous, the whole world being against it, that it was come to the last extremity. Noah's reproofs, and his preaching of righteousness, were utterly disregarded. God's Spirit had striven with them a hundred and twenty years, but all in vain; and the church was reduced to so narrow limits, as to be confined to one family. There was no prospect of anything else but of their totally swallowing up the church, and that in a very little time; and so wholly destroying that small root that had the blessing in it, whence the Redeemer was to proceed.

And therefore, God's destroying those enemies of the church by the flood belongs to this affair of redemption; for it was one thing that was done in fulfilment of the covenant of grace, as it was revealed to Adam: "I will put enmity between thee and the woman, and between thy seed and her seed; it shall bruise thy head." This was only a destruction of the seed of the serpent in the midst of their most violent rage against the seed of the woman, when in the utmost peril by them.

We read in Scripture of scarce any destruction of nations but that one main reason given for it is, their enmity and injuries against God's church; and doubtless this was one main reason of the destruction of all nations by the flood. The giants that were in those days, in all likelihood, got themselves renown by their great exploits against heaven, and against Christ and his church, the remaining sons of God that had not corrupted themselves.

We read, that just before the world shall be destroyed by fire,

> the nations that are in the four quarters of the earth, shall gather together against the church as the sand of the sea, and shall go up on the breadth of the earth, and compass the camp of the saints about, and the beloved city; and then fire shall come down from God out of heaven, and devour them. (Rev. 20:8-9).

And it seems there was that which was very parallel to it, just before the world was destroyed by water. And, therefore, their destruction was a work of God that did as much belong to the work of redemption, as the destruction of the Egyptians belonged to the redemption of the children of Israel out of Egypt, or as the destruction of Sennacherib's mighty army, that had compassed

about Jerusalem to destroy it, belonged to God's redemption of that city from them.

By means of this flood, all the enemies of God's
church, against whom that little handful had no strength,
were swept off at once. God took their part, appeared
for them against their enemies, and drowned those of
whom they had been afraid, in the flood of water, as
he drowned the enemies of Israel that pursued them in
the Red Sea.

Indeed, God could have taken other methods to
deliver his church: he could have converted all the world
instead of drowning it; and so, he could have taken
another method than drowning the Egyptians in the
Red Sea. But that is no argument, that the method he
did take, was not a method to show his redeeming mercy
to them.

By the deluge the enemies of God's people were
dispossessed of the earth, and the whole earth was given
to Noah and his family to possess it in quiet; as God
made room for the Israelites in Canaan, by casting out
their enemies from before them. And God thus taking
the possession of the enemies of the church, and giving
it all to his church, was agreeable to that promise of the
covenant of grace: Ps. 37: 9-11,

> For evil-doers shall be cut off: but those that wait upon
> the Lord, they shall inherit the earth. For yet a little while
> and the wicked shall not be: yea, thou shalt diligently
> consider his place, and it shall not be. But the meek
> shall inherit the earth, and shall delight themselves in
> the abundance of peace.

**II.** Another thing belonging to the same work, was God's wonderfully preserving that family of which the Redeemer was to proceed, when all the rest of the world was drowned. God's drowning the world, and saving Noah and his family, were both reducible to this great work. The saving of Noah and his family belonged to it two ways, viz. as from that family the Redeemer was to proceed, and it was the mystical body of Christ that was there saved. The manner of saving those persons, when all the world besides was so overthrown, was very wonderful. It was a wonderful type of the redemption of Christ, of that redemption that is sealed by the baptism of water, and is so spoken of in the New Testament, as 1 Pet. 3:20-21,

> Which sometimes were disobedient, when once the long-suffering of God waited in the days of Noah, while the ark was a preparing, wherein few, that is, eight souls, were saved by water. The like figure whereunto, even baptism, doth also now save us, (not the putting away of the filth of the flesh, but the answer of a good conscience towards God,) by the resurrection of Jesus Christ.

That water which washed away the filth of the world, that cleared the world of wicked men, was a type of the blood of Christ, that takes away the sin of the world. That water which delivered Noah and his sons from their enemies, is a type of the blood that delivers God's church from their sins, their worst enemies. That water, which was so plentiful and abundant, that it filled the world, and reached above the tops of the highest mountains, was a type of that blood, which is sufficient for the whole world; sufficient to bury the highest mountains of sin. The ark, that was the refuge and hiding-place of the church in this time of storm and flood, was a type of Christ, the true hiding-place of the church from the storms and floods of God's wrath.

**III.** The next thing I would observe is, the new grant of the earth God made to Noah and his family immediately after the flood, as founded on the covenant of grace. The sacrifice of Christ was represented by Noah's building an altar to the Lord, and offering a sacrifice of every clean beast, and every clean fowl. And we have an account of God accepting this sacrifice: and thereupon he blessed Noah, and established his covenant with him, and with his seed, promising to destroy the earth in like manner no more; signifying that it is by the sacrifice of Christ, God's favour is obtained, and his people are in safety from destroying judgments, and obtain the blessing of the Lord. And God now, on occasion of this sacrifice that Noah offered, gives him and his posterity a new grant of the earth; a new power of dominion over the creatures, as founded on that sacrifice, and so founded on the covenant of grace. And so, it is to be looked upon as a different grant from that which was made to Adam, Gen. 1:28,

> And God blessed them, and God said unto them, Be fruitful, and multiply, and replenish the earth, and subdue it; and have dominion over the fish of the sea, and over the fowl of the air, and over every living thing that moveth upon the earth.

That grant was not founded on the covenant of grace; for it was given to Adam while he was under the covenant of works, and therefore was antiquated when that covenant ceased. Hence it came to pass, that the earth was taken away from mankind by the flood: for the first grant was forfeited; and God had never made another after that, till after the flood. If the first covenant had not been broken, God never would have drowned the world, and so have taken it away from mankind; for then the first grant made to mankind would have stood good. But that being broken, God after a while destroyed the earth, when the wickedness of man was great.

But after the flood, on Noah's offering a sacrifice that represented the sacrifice of Christ, God in smelling a sweet savour, or accepting the sacrifice – as it was a representation of the true sacrifice of Christ, which is a sweet savour indeed to God – gives Noah a new grant of the earth, founded on that covenant of grace which is by the sacrifice of Christ, with a promise annexed, that now the earth should no more be destroyed, till the consummation of all things; (Gen. 8:20-22; 9:1-3, 7.) The reason why such a promise, that God would no more destroy the earth, was added to this grant made to Noah, and not to that made to Adam, was because this was founded on the covenant of grace, of which Christ was the surety, and therefore could not be broken. And therefore it comes to pass now, that though the wickedness of man has dreadfully raged, and the earth has been filled with violence and wickedness, one age after another, and much more dreadful and aggravated wickedness, being against so much greater light and mercy; especially in these days of the gospel: yet God's patience holds out; God does not destroy the earth: his mercy and forbearance abides according to his promise; and his grant established with Noah and his sons abides firm and good, being founded on the covenant of grace.

**IV.** On this, God renews with Noah and his sons the covenant of grace, Gen. 9:9-10. "And I, behold, I establish my covenant with you, and with your seed after you, and with every living creature that is with you," etc.; which was the covenant of grace; of which even the brute creation have this as benefit, that it shall never be destroyed again until the consummation of all things. By this expression in Scripture, "my covenant," is commonly to be understood the covenant of grace. The manner of expression, I will establish my covenant with you, and with your seed after you, shows plainly, that it was a covenant already in being, and that Noah would understand by that denomination the covenant of grace.

**V.** God's disappointing the design of building the city and tower of Babel belongs to the great work of redemption. For that building was undertaken in opposition of this great building of God of which we are speaking. Men's going about to build such a city and tower was an effect of the corruption into which mankind were now fallen. This city and tower were set up in opposition to the city of God, as the god to whom they built it, was their pride. Being sunk into a disposition to forsake the true God, the first idol they set up in his room, was their own fame. And as this city and tower had their foundation laid in the pride and vanity of men, and the haughtiness of their minds, so it was built on a foundation exceedingly contrary to the nature of the kingdom of Christ, and his redeemed city, which has its foundation laid in humility.

Therefore, God saw that it tended to frustrate the design of that great building which was founded in Christ's humiliation: and therefore, the thing displeased the Lord, and he baffled and confounded the design. God will frustrate and confound all other designs, that are set up in opposition to the great work of redemption.

Isaiah 2, representing God setting up the kingdom of Christ in the world, foretells how, in order to it, he will bring down the haughtiness of men, and how the day of the Lord shall be on every high tower, and upon every fenced wall, etc. Christ's kingdom is established, by bringing down every high thing to make way for it, 2 Cor. 10:4-5,

> For the weapons of our warfare are mighty through God, to the pulling down of strong holds, casting down imaginations, and every high thing that exalteth itself against the knowledge of God.

What is done in a particular soul, to make way for the setting up of Christ's kingdom, is to destroy Babel in that soul.

They intended to have built Babel up to heaven. However, that building of which we speak shall reach to heaven indeed, the highest heavens, at the end of the world, when it shall be finished: and therefore, God would not suffer the building of his enemies, in opposition to it, to prosper. If they had prospered in building that city and tower, it might have kept the world of wicked men, the enemies of the church, together, as that was their design. They might have remained united in one vast, powerful city; and so have been too powerful for the city of God.

This Babel is the same with the city of Babylon; for Babylon in the original is Babel. But Babylon is always spoken of in Scripture as chiefly opposite to the city of God, as a powerful and terrible enemy, notwithstanding this great check put to the building of it in the beginning. But it probably would have been vastly more powerful, and able to vex if not to destroy the church of God, if it had not been thus checked.

Thus, it was in kindness to his church, and in prosecution of the great design of redemption, that God put a stop to the building of the city and tower of Babel.

**VI.** The dispersing of the nations, and dividing the earth among its inhabitants, immediately after God had caused the building of Babel to cease. This was done so as most to suit the great design of redemption. And particularly, God therein had an eye to the future propagation of the gospel among the nations. They were so placed, their habitation so limited, round about the land of Canaan, as most suited that design. Deut. 32:8, "When the Most High divided to the nations their inheritance, when he separated the sons of Adam, he set the bounds of the people according to the number of the children of Israel." Acts 17:26-27,

> And hath made of one blood all nations of men, for to dwell on all the face of the earth, and hath determined the times before appointed, and the bounds of their habitation; that they should seek the Lord, if happily they might feel after him, and find him.

The land of Canaan was the most conveniently situated of any place in the world, for the purpose of spreading revealed light among the nations in general. The Roman empire, the chief part of the civilized world, in the apostolic age, was in the countries round about Jerusalem. The devil, seeing the advantage of this situation of the nations for promoting the great work of redemption, and the disadvantage of it with respect to the interests of his kingdom, afterward led away many nations into the remotest parts of the world, to get them out of the way of the gospel. Thus, he led some into America; and others into northern cold regions, that are almost inaccessible.

**VII.** Another thing I would mention in this period, was God's preserving the true religion in that line from which Christ was to proceed, when the world in general apostatized to idolatry, and the church was in imminent danger of being swallowed in the general corruption. Although God had lately wrought so wonderfully for the deliverance of his church, and had shown so great mercy towards it, as for its sake even to destroy all the rest of the world; and although he had lately renewed and established his covenant of grace with Noah and his sons; yet so prone is the corrupt heart of man to depart from God, and to sink into the depths of wickedness, darkness, and delusion, that the world soon after the flood fell into gross idolatry; so that before Abraham the distemper had become almost universal. The earth had become very corrupt at the time of the building of Babel; even God's people themselves, that line of which Christ was to come. Josh. 24:2, "Your fathers dwelt on the other side of the flood in old time, even Terah the father of Abraham, and the father of Nahor; and they served other gods." The other side of the flood means beyond the river Euphrates, where the ancestors of Abraham lived.

We are not to understand, that they were wholly drawn off to idolatry, to forsake the true God. For God is said to be the God of Nahor: Gen. 31:53, "The God of Abraham, and the God of Nahor, the God of their father, judge betwixt us." But they partook in some measure of the general and almost universal corruption of the times; as Solomon was in a measure infected with idolatrous corruption; and as the children of Israel in Egypt are said to serve other gods, though there was the true church of God among them; and as there were images kept for a considerable time in the family of Jacob, the corruption being brought from Padan-Aram, whence he fetched his wives.

This was the second time that the church was almost brought to nothing by the corruption and general defection of the world from true religion. But still the true religion was kept up in the family from which Christ was to proceed. Which is another instance of God's remarkably preserving his church in a time of a general deluge of wickedness; and wherein, although the god of this world raged, and had almost swallowed up God's church, yet he did not suffer the gates of hell to prevail against it.

## 1.3 PART III
### 4.0 From the Calling of Abraham to Moses

I PROCEED NOW to show how the work of redemption was carried on from the calling of Abraham to Moses.

**I.** And it pleased God now to separate that person of whom Christ was to come, from the rest of the world, that his church might be upheld in his family and posterity till that time. He called Abraham out of his own country, and from his kindred, to go into a distant country, that God should show him; and brought him first out of Ur of the Chaldees to Charran, and then to the land of Canaan.

It was before observed, that the idolatrous corruption of the world had now become general; mankind were almost wholly overrun with idolatry. God therefore saw it necessary, in order to uphold true religion in the world, that there should be a family separated from all others. It proved to be high time to take this course, lest the church of Christ should wholly be carried away with the apostacy. For Abraham's own country and kindred had most of them fallen off; and without some extraordinary interposition of Providence, in all likelihood, in a generation or two more, the true religion in this line would have been extinct. And, therefore, God called Abraham, the person in whose family he intended to uphold the true religion, out of his own country, and from his kindred, to a far distant country, that his posterity might there remain a people separate from all the rest of the world; that so the true religion might be upheld there, while all mankind besides were swallowed up in heathenism.

The land of the Chaldees, whence Abraham was called, was the country about Babel. Babel, or Babylon, was the chief city of Chaldea. Learned men suppose by what they gather from the most ancient accounts of things, that it was in this land that idolatry first began; that Babel and Chaldea were the original and chief seats of the worship of idols, whence it spread into other nations. And therefore the land of the Chaldeans, the country of Babylon, is in Scripture called the land of graven images; Jer. 1:35, 38,

> A sword is upon the Chaldeans, saith the Lord, and upon the inhabitants of Babylon, and upon her princes, and upon her wise men. – A drought is upon her waters, and they shall be dried up; for it is the land of graven images, and they are mad upon their idols.

God calls Abraham out of this idolatrous country, to a great distance from it. And when he came there, he gave him no inheritance in it, no not so much as to set his foot on; but he remained a stranger and a sojourner, that he and his family might be kept separate from all the world.

This was a new thing: God had never taken such a method before. His church had not in this manner been separated from the rest of the world till now; but were wont to dwell with them, without any bar or fence to keep them separate; the mischievous consequence of which had been found once and again. Before the flood, the effect of God's people living intermingled with the wicked world, without any remarkable wall of separation, was, that the sons of the church joined in marriage with others, and thereby almost all soon became infected, and the church was almost brought to nothing. The method that God then took to fence the church was, to drown the wicked world, and save the church in the ark. Before Abraham was called, the world had become corrupt again. But now God took another method; he did not destroy the wicked world, and save Abraham, and his wife, and Lot, but calls these persons to go and live separate from the rest of the world.

This was a new and great thing, that God did toward the work of redemption. It was about the middle of the space of time between the fall of man and the coming of Christ; about two thousand years before the great Redeemer was to appear. But by this calling of Abraham, the ancestor of Christ, a foundation was laid for upholding the church in the world, till Christ should come. For the world having become idolatrous, there was a necessity in order to this, that the seed of the woman should be thus separated from it.

And then it was needful that there should be a particular nation separated from the rest of the world, to receive the types and prophecies that were to be given of Christ, to prepare the way for his coming; that to them might be committed the oracles of God; that by them the history of God's great works of creation and providence might be preserved; that Christ might be born of this nation; and that from hence the light of the gospel might shine forth to the rest of the world. These ends could not well be obtained, if God's people, through all these two thousand years, had lived intermixed with the heathen world. So that the calling of Abraham may be looked upon as a kind of new foundation laid for the visible church of God, in a more distinct and regular state. Abraham, being the person in whom this foundation is laid, is represented in Scripture as though he were the father of all the church, the father of all them that believe; a root whence the visible church rose as a tree, distinct from all other plants. Of this tree Christ was the branch of righteousness; and from it, after Christ came, the natural branches were broken off, and the Gentiles were grafted in. So that Abraham still remains the father, the root of the church. It is the same tree which, from that small beginning in Abraham's time, has in these days of the gospel spread its branches over a great part of the earth, and will fill the whole in due time, and at the end of the world shall be transplanted from an earthly soil into the paradise of God.

**II.** There accompanied this a more particular and full revelation and confirmation of the covenant of grace than ever before. There had been, before this, two particular and solemn editions or confirmations of this covenant; one, to our first parents, soon after the fall; the other, to Noah and his family, soon after the flood. And now there is a third, at and after the calling of Abraham. It is now revealed to Abraham, not only that Christ should come; but that he should be his seed; and promised, that all the families of the earth should be blessed in him. And God repeated the promises of this to Abraham. The first promise was when he first called him, Gen. 11:2, "And I will make of thee a great nation, and I will bless thee, and make thy name great; and thou shalt be a blessing." The same promise was renewed after he came into the land of Canaan, (Gen. 13:14-17). Again after Abraham had returned from the slaughter of the kings (Gen. 15:5-6). And a fourth time, after his offering up Isaac (Gen. 12:16-18).

In this renewal of the covenant of grace with Abraham, several particulars concerning it were revealed more fully than before; not only that Christ was to be of Abraham's seed, but also, the calling of the Gentiles, that all nations should be brought into the church, all the families of the earth made blessed. And then the great condition of the covenant of grace, which is faith, was now more fully made known. Gen. 15:5-6, "And he said unto him, So shall thy seed be. And Abraham believed God, and it was counted unto him for righteousness."

Which is much noticed in the New Testament, as that for which Abraham was called the father of believers.

And as there was now a further revelation of the covenant of grace, so there was a further confirmation of it by seals and pledges; particularly, circumcision, which was a seal of the covenant of grace, as appears by the first institution of it, Gen. 17. It there pappears to be a seal of that covenant by which God promised to make Abraham a father of many nations (Gen. 17:5, 9, 10). And we are expressly taught, that it was a seal of righteousness of faith, Rom. 4:11. Speaking of Abraham, the apostle says, he received the sign of circumcision, a seal of the righteousness of faith.

Abraham's family and posterity must be kept separate from the rest of the world, till Christ should come; and this sacrament was the principal wall of separation. Besides, God gave Abraham a remarkable pledge of the fulfilment of the promise he had made him, in his victory over Chedorlaomer and the kings that were with him. Chedorlaomer seems to have been a great emperor, who reigned over a great part of the world at that day; and though he had his seat at Elam, which was not much, if anything, short of a thousand miles distant from the land of Canaan, yet he extended his empire so as to reign over many parts of the land of Canaan, as it appears by Gen. 14:4-7. It is supposed by learned men, that he was a king of the Assyrian empire at that day, which had been before begun by Nimrod at Babel. And as it was the honour of kings in those days to build cities for the seat of their empire (Gen. 10:10-12), so it is conjectured, that he had gone forth and built him a city in Elam, and made that his seat; and that those other kings who came with him, were his deputies in the several cities and countries where they reigned. But yet as mighty an empire as he had, and as great an army as he came with, Abraham, only with his trained servants, that were born in his house, conquered and subdued this mighty emperor, the kings that came with him, and all their army. This he received of God as a pledge of what he had promised, viz. the victory that Christ his seed should obtain over the nations of the earth, whereby he should possess the gates of his enemies. It is plainly spoken of as such in the 41st of Isaiah. In that chapter is it foretold of that future glorious victory the church shall obtain over the nations of the world (Isa. 41:1, 10, 15). This victory of Abraham over such a great emperor and his mighty forces, is spoken of as a pledge and earnest of victory to the church, Isa. 41:2-3,

> Who raised up the righteous man from the east, called him to his foot, gave the nations before him, and made him rule over kings? He gave them as the dust to his sword, and as driven stubble to his bow. He pursued them, and passed safely; even by the way that he had not gone with his feet.

Another remarkable confirmation Abraham received of the covenant of grace was when he returned from the slaughter of the kings; when Melchizedek the king of Salem, the priest of the most high God, that great type of Christ, met him, and blessed him, and brought forth bread and wine. The bread and wine signified the same blessings of the covenant of grace that the bread and wine does in the sacrament of the Lord's supper. As Abraham had a seal of the covenant in circumcision that was equivalent to baptism, so now he had a seal of it equivalent to the Lord's supper. And Melchizedek's coming to meet him with such a seal of the covenant of grace, on the occasion of this victory, evidences that it was a pledge of God's fulfilment of the same covenant (Gen. 14:19-20).

Another confirmation of the covenant of grace, was the vision he had, in the deep sleep that fell upon him, of the smoking furnace, and burning lamp, that passed between the parts of the sacrifice (Gen. 15). The sacrifice signified that of Christ. The smoking furnace that passed through the midst of that sacrifice first signified the sufferings of Christ. But the burning lamp that followed, which shone with a clear bright light, signifies the glory that followed Christ's sufferings, and what was procured by them.

Another remarkable pledge that God gave Abraham of the fulfilment of the covenant of grace was his giving of that child of whom Christ was to come in his old age (Heb. 11:11-12 and Rom. 4:18-25), and his delivering Isaac, after he was laid upon the wood of the sacrifice to be slain. This was a confirmation of Abraham's faith in the promise that God had made of Christ, that he should be of Isaac's posterity; and was a representation of the resurrection of Christ (Heb. 11:17-19). And because this was given as a confirmation of the covenant of grace, therefore God renewed that covenant with Abraham on this occasion (Gen. 22:15-18).

Thus, you see how much more fully the covenant of grace was revealed and confirmed in Abraham's time than ever it had been before; by means of which Abraham seems to have had a clear view of Christ the great Redeemer, and the future things that were to be accomplished by him. And, therefore, Christ informs us, that "Abraham rejoiced to see his day, and he saw it and was glad" (John 8:56). So great an advance did it please God now to make in this building, which he had been carrying on from the beginning of the world.

**III.** The next thing is God's preserving the patriarchs for so long a time in the midst of the wicked inhabitants of Canaan, and from all other enemies. The patriarchs, Abraham, Isaac, and Jacob were those of whom Christ was to proceed; and they were now separated from the world, that in them his church might be upheld. Therefore, in preserving them, the great design of redemption was carried on. He preserved them, and kept the inhabitants of the land where they sojourned from destroying them; which was a remarkable dispensation of providence. For the inhabitants of the land were at that day very wicked, though they grew more wicked afterwards. This appears by Gen. 15:16, "In the fourth generation they shall come hither again; for the iniquity of the Canaanites is not yet full", as much as to say, though it be very great, yet it is not yet full. And their great wickedness also appears by Abraham and Isaac's aversion to their children marrying any of the daughters of the land. Abraham, when he was old, could not be content till he had made his servant swear that he would not take a wife for his son of the daughters of the land. And Isaac and Rebecca were content to send away Jacob to so great a distance as Padan-Aram, to take him a wife thence. And when Esau married some of the daughters of the land, we are told, that they were a grief of mind to Isaac and Rebecca.

Another argument of their great wickedness, was the instances we have in Sodom and Gomorrah, Admah and Zeboim, which were some of the cities of Canaan, though they were probably most notoriously wicked; and likely to have the most bitter enmity against these holy men; agreeable to what was declared at first, "I will put enmity between thee and the woman, and between thy seed and her seed." Their holy lives were a continual condemnation of their wickedness. Besides, it could not be otherwise, but that they must be much in reproving their wickedness, as we find Lot was in Sodom; who, we are told, vexed his righteous soul with their unlawful deeds, and was to them a preacher of righteousness.

And they were the more exposed to them, being strangers and sojourners in the land, and having as yet no inheritance there. Men are more apt to find fault with strangers, and to be irritated by anything in them that offends, as they were with Lot in Sodom. He very gently reproved their wickedness; and they say upon it, "This fellow came in to sojourn, and he will needs be a ruler and a judge" and threatened what they would do to him.

But God wonderfully preserved Abraham and Lot, Isaac and Jacob, and their families, amongst them, though they were few in number, and they might quickly have destroyed them; which is taken notice of as a wonderful instance of God's preserving mercy towards his church, Psalm 105:12-15:

> When they were but a few men in number; yea, very few, and strangers in it. When they went from one nation to another, from one kingdom to another people. He suffered no man to do them wrong; yea, he reproved kings for their sakes, saying, Touch not mine anointed, and do my prophets no harm.

This preservation was, in some instances especially, very remarkable; when the people of the land were greatly irritated and provoked; as they were by Simeon and Levi's treatment of the Shechemites, in Gen. 34:30-31. God then strangely preserved Jacob and his family, restraining the provoked people by an unusual terror on their minds. Gen. 35:5, "And the terror of God was upon the cities that were round about them, and they did not pursue after the sons of Jacob."

And God preserved them, not only from the Canaanites, but from all others that intended mischief to them. He preserved Jacob and his company, when pursued by Laban, full of rage, and a disposition to overtake, him as an enemy. God met him, rebuked him, and said to him, "Take heed that thou speak not to Jacob either good or bad." How wonderfully did he also preserve him from Esau his brother, when he came forth with an army, with a full design to cut him off! How did God, in answer to his prayer, when Jacob wrestled with Christ at Penuel, wonderfully turn Esau's heart, and make him, instead of meeting him as an enemy with slaughter and destruction, to meet him as a friend and brother, doing him no harm!

And thus was this handful, this little root that had the blessing of the Redeemer in it, preserved in the midst of enemies and dangers: which was not unlike to preserving the ark in the midst of the tempestuous deluge.

**IV.** The next thing I would mention is, the awful destruction of Sodom and Gomorrah, and the neighbouring cities. This tended to promote the great work designed two ways: First, as it tended powerfully to restrain the inhabitants of the land from injuring those holy strangers that God had brought to sojourn amongst them. Lot was one of those strangers; he came into the land with Abraham; and Sodom was destroyed for their abusive disregard of Lot, the preacher of righteousness. And their destruction came upon their committing a most injurious and abominable insult on Lot, and the strangers that had come into his house, even those angels, whom they probably took to be some of Lot's former acquaintance that had come to visit him. They in a most outrageous manner beset Lot's house, intending a monstrous abuse and act of violence on those strangers, and threatening to serve Lot worse than them.

But in the midst of this, God smote them with blindness; and the next morning the city and the country about it was overthrown in a most terrible storm of fire and brimstone; with dreadful destruction, as it was in the sight of the rest of the inhabitants of the land, and therefore greatly tended to restrain them from hurting those holy strangers anymore; it doubtless struck a dread and terror on their minds, and made them afraid to hurt them, and probably was one principal means to restrain them, and preserve the patriarchs. And when that reason is given, why the inhabitants of the land did not pursue after Jacob, when they were so provoked by the destruction of the Shechemites, viz. that the terror of the Lord was upon them; it is very probable, that this was the terror which was set home upon them. They remembered the amazing destruction of Sodom, and the cities of the plain, that came upon them for their abusive treatment of Lot, and so durst not hurt Jacob and his family, though they were so much provoked to it.

Another way that this awful destruction tended to promote this great affair of redemption, was, that hereby God remarkably exhibited the terrors of his law, to make men sensible of their need of redeeming mercy. The work of redemption never was carried on without this. The law, from the beginning, is made use of as a schoolmaster to bring men to Christ.

But under the Old Testament there was much more need of some extraordinary, visible, and sensible manifestation of God's wrath against sin than in the days of the gospel; since a future state, and the eternal misery of hell, is more clearly revealed, and since the awful justice of God against the sins of men has been so wonderfully displayed in the sufferings of Christ. And, therefore, the revelation that God gave of himself in those days, used to be accompanied with much more terror than it is in these days of the gospel. So, when God appeared at mount Sinai to give the law, it was with thunders and lightnings, and a thick cloud, and the voice of the trumpet exceeding loud. Some external, awful manifestations of God's wrath against sin were on some accounts especially necessary before the giving of the law: and therefore, before the flood, the terrors of the law handed down by tradition from Adam served for that purpose. Adam lived nine hundred and thirty years himself, to proclaim God's awful threatenings denounced in the covenant made with him, and how dreadful the consequences of the fall were; and others, that conversed with Adam, lived till the flood. And the destruction of the world by the flood served to exhibit the terrors of the law, and manifested the wrath of God against sin; in order to make men sensible of the absolute necessity of redeeming mercy. And some that saw the flood were alive in Abraham's time.

But this was now in a great measure forgotten; therefore God was pleased again, in a most amazing manner, to show his wrath against sin, in the destruction of these cities; which was the liveliest image of hell of any thing that ever had been; and therefore the apostle Jude says, "They suffer the vengeance of eternal fire," Jude 7. God rained storms of fire and brimstone upon them; probably by thick flashes of lightning. The streams of brimstone burnt up all these cities; so that they perished in the flames of divine wrath. That by this might be seen the dreadful wrath of God against the ungodliness and unrighteousness of men; which tended to show the necessity of redemption, and so to promote that great work.

**V.** God again renewed and confirmed the covenant of grace to Isaac and Jacob. To Isaac in these words; Gen. 26:3-4:

> "And I will perform the oath which I sware unto Abraham thy father; and I will make thy seed to multiply as the stars of heaven, and will give unto thy seed all these countries; and in thy seed shall all the nations of the earth be blessed."

And afterwards to Jacob; first, in Isaac blessing him and his seed, wherein he acted and spoke by extraordinary divine direction, Gen. 27:29:

> "Let people serve thee, and nations bow down to thee; be lord over thy brethren, and let thy mother's sons bow down to thee: Cursed be every one that curseth thee, and blessed be he that blesseth thee."

And therefore Esau, not included in this blessing, missed of being blessed as an heir of the benefits of the covenant of grace.

This covenant was again renewed and confirmed to Jacob at Bethel, in his vision of the ladder that reached to heaven; which was a symbol of the way of salvation by Christ. The stone that Jacob rested on was a type of Christ, the stone of Israel, which the spiritual Israel rests upon; as is evident, because it was anointed, and made use of as an altar. But we know that Christ is the anointed of God, and is the only true altar. While Jacob was resting on this stone, and saw this ladder, God appears to him as his covenant God, and renews the covenant of grace with him; as in Gen. 28:14:

> "And thy seed shall be as the dust of the earth; and thou shalt spread abroad to the west, and to the east, and to the north, and to the south; and in thee and in thy seed shall all the families of the earth be blessed."

Jacob had another remarkable confirmation of this covenant at Penuel, where he wrestled with God, and prevailed; where Christ appeared to him in the form of that nature which he was afterwards to receive in a personal union with his divine nature. And God renewed his covenant with him again, after he left Padan-Aram, and had come up to Bethel, and where he had the vision of the ladder; as you may see in Gen. 35:10-15.

Thus, the covenant of grace was now renewed much oftener than it had been before. The light of the gospel now began to shine much brighter, as the time of Christ's appearing drew nearer.

**VI.** The next thing I would observe, is God's remarkable preservation of the family – of which Christ was to proceed – from perishing by famine, by the instrumentality of Joseph. When there was a seven-years famine approaching, God was pleased, by a wonderful providence, to send Joseph into Egypt, there to provide for Jacob and his family, and to keep the holy seed alive, which otherwise would have perished. Joseph was sent into Egypt for that end, as he observes, Gen. 1:20, "But as for you, ye thought evil against me; but God meant it unto good, to save much people alive." How often had this holy root, that had in it the future branch of righteousness, the glorious Redeemer, been in danger of being destroyed! But God wonderfully preserved it.

This salvation of the house of Israel, by the hand of Joseph, was upon some accounts very much a resemblance of the salvation of Christ. The children of Israel were saved by Joseph their kinsman and brother, from perishing by famine; as he that saves the souls of the spiritual Israel from spiritual famine is their near kinsman, and one that is not ashamed to call them brethren. Joseph was a brother they had hated, sold, and had it as if he were killed; for they had designed to kill him. So, Christ is one that we naturally hate, and by our wicked lives, have sold for the vain things of the world, and by our sins have slain. Joseph was first in a state of humiliation; he was a servant, as Christ appeared in the form of a servant; and then was cast into a dungeon, as Christ descended into the grave. When he rose out of the dungeon, he was in a state of great exaltation, at the king's right hand as his deputy, to reign over all his kingdom, to provide food, to preserve life; and being in this state of exaltation, he dispenses food to his brethren, and so gives them life. So, Christ was exalted at God's right hand to be a Prince and Saviour to his brethren, received gifts for men, even for the rebellious, them that had hated and sold him.

**VII.** After this there was a prophecy of Christ, on some accounts more particular than any before, in Jacob's blessing his son Judah. This was more particular as it showed of whose posterity he was to be. When God called Abraham, it was revealed that he was to be of Abraham's posterity. Before, we have no account of any revelation concerning Christ's pedigree confined to narrower limits than the posterity of Noah: after this it was confined to still narrower limits; for though Abraham had many sons, yet it was revealed, that Christ was to be of Isaac's posterity. And then it was limited still more; for when Isaac had two sons, it was revealed that Christ was to be of Israel's posterity. And now, though Israel had twelve sons, yet it is revealed that Christ should be of Judah's posterity. Christ is the lion of the tribe of Judah. Respect is chiefly had to his great acts, when it is said here, Gen. 49:8,

> Judah, thou art he whom thy brethren shall praise; thy hand shall be in the neck of thine enemies; thy father's children shall bow down before thee. Judah is a lion's whelp; from the prey, my son, thou art gone up: he stooped down, he couched as a lion, and as an old lion; who shall rouse him up?

And then this prediction is more particular concerning the time of Christ's coming, as in Gen. 49:10,

> The sceptre shall not depart from Judah, nor a lawgiver from between his feet, until Shiloh come; and unto him shall the gathering of the people be.

The prophecy here, of the calling of the Gentiles consequent on Christ's coming, seems to be more plain than any had been before, in the expression, "to him shall the gathering of the people be." Thus you see how that gospel-light which dawned immediately after the fall of man, gradually increases.

**VIII.** The work of redemption was carried on in this period, in God's wonderfully preserving the children of Israel in Egypt, when the power of Egypt was engaged utterly to destroy them. They seemed to be wholly in the hands of the Egyptians; they were their servants, and were subject to the power of Pharaoh: and Pharaoh set himself to weaken them with hard bondage. And when he saw that did not, he set himself to extirpate their race, by commanding that every male child should be drowned. But after all that Pharaoh could do, God wonderfully preserved them; and not only so, but increased them exceedingly; so that, instead of being extirpated, they greatly multiplied.

**IX.** Here is to be observed, not only the preservation of the nation, but God's wonderfully preserving and upholding his invisible church in that nation, when in danger of being overwhelmed by the idolatry of Egypt. The children of Israel being long among the Egyptians, and servants under them, and so not having advantages to keep God's ordinances among themselves, and maintain any public worship or instruction, whereby the true religion might be upheld, and there being now no written word, they by degrees, in a great measure, lost the true religion, and borrowed the idolatry of Egypt; and the greater part of the people fell away to the worship of their gods. This we learn by Ezek. 20:6-8; 23:8.

This now was the third time that God's church was almost swallowed up and carried away with the wickedness of the world; once before the flood; the other time, before the calling of Abraham; and now, the third time, in Egypt. But yet God did not suffer his church to be quite overwhelmed: he still saved it, like the ark in the flood, and as he saved Moses in the midst of the waters, in an ark of bulrushes, where he was in the utmost danger of being swallowed up. The true religion was still kept up with some; and God had still a people among them, even in this miserable, corrupt, and dark time. The parents of Moses were true servants of God, as we may see by Heb. 11:23, "By faith Moses, when he was born, was hid three months of his parents, because they saw that he was a proper child; and they were not afraid of the king's commandment."

I have now shown how the work of redemption was carried on from the calling of Abraham to Moses; in which we have seen many great things done towards this work, and a great advancement of this building, beyond what had preceded.

## 1.4 PART IV

### 5.0 From Moses to David

I PROCEED TO THE TIME which reaches from Moses to David.

**I.** The first thing that offers itself is the redemption of the church of God out of Egypt; the most remarkable of all in the Old Testament, the greatest pledge and forerunner of the future redemption by Christ, and much more insisted on in Scripture than any other of those redemptions. And indeed it was the greatest type of Christ's redemption of any providential event whatsoever. This was by Jesus Christ, for it was wrought by him who appeared to Moses in the bush; the person that sent Moses to redeem that people. But that was Christ, as is evident, because he is called the angel of the Lord, Exod. 3:2-3. The bush represented the human nature of Christ, who is called the branch. This bush grew on mount Sinai or Horeb, a word that signifies a dry place, as the human nature of Christ was a root out of a dry ground. The bush burning with fire, represented the sufferings of Christ, in the fire of God's wrath. It burned, and was not consumed; so Christ, though he suffered extremely, yet perished not; but overcame at last, and rose from his sufferings. Because this great mystery of the incarnation and sufferings of Christ was here represented, therefore Moses says, I will turn aside, and behold this great sight. A great sight he might well call it, when there was represented, God manifest in the flesh, suffering a dreadful death, and rising from the dead.

This was the glorious Redeemer who redeemed the church out of Egypt, from under the hand of Pharaoh; as Christ, by his death and sufferings, redeemed his people from Satan, the spiritual Pharaoh. He redeemed them from hard service and cruel drudgery; so Christ redeems his people from the cruel slavery of sin and Satan. He redeemed them, as it is said, from the iron furnace; so Christ redeems his church from a furnace of fire and everlasting burnings. – He redeemed them with a strong hand and outstretched arm, and great and terrible judgments on their enemies; so Christ with mighty power triumphs over principalities and powers, and executes terrible judgments on his church's enemies, bruising the serpent's head. He saved them, when others were destroyed, by the sprinkling of the blood of the paschal lamb; so God's church is saved from death by the sprinkling of the blood of Christ, when the rest of the world is destroyed. God brought forth the people sorely against the will of the Egyptians, when they could not bear to let them go; so Christ rescues his people out of the hands of the devil, sorely against his will, when his proud heart cannot bear to be overcome.

In that redemption, Christ did not only redeem the people from the Egyptians, but he redeemed them from the devils, the gods of Egypt; for before, they had been in a state of servitude to the gods of Egypt, as well as to the men. And Christ, the seed of the woman, did now, in a very remarkable manner, fulfill the curse on the serpent, in bruising his head: Exod. 12:12. "For I will pass through the land of Egypt this night, and will smite all the first-born in the land of Egypt, both man and beast, and against all the gods of Egypt will I execute judgment." Hell was as much, nay more engaged in that affair, than Egypt was. The pride and cruelty of

Satan, that old serpent, was more concerned in it than Pharaoh's. He did his utmost against the people, and to his utmost opposed their redemption. But it is said, that when God redeemed his people out of Egypt, he "broke the heads of the dragons in the waters, and broke the head of leviathan in pieces, and gave him to be meat for the people inhabiting the wilderness," Ps. 74:12-14. God forced their enemies to let them go, that they might serve him; as Zacharias observes with respect to the church under the gospel, Luke 1:74-5.

The people of Israel went out with a high hand, and Christ went before them in a pillar of cloud and fire. There was a glorious triumph over earth and hell in that deliverance. When Pharaoh and his hosts, and Satan by them, pursued the people, Christ overthrew them in the Red Sea; the Lord triumphed gloriously; the horse and his rider he cast into the sea, and there they slept their sleep, and never followed the children of Israel anymore. The Red Sea represented Christ's blood, because the apostle compares the children of Israel's passage through the Red Sea to baptism, 1 Cor. 10:1-2. – But we all know that the water of baptism represents Christ's blood.

Thus Christ, the angel of God's presence, in his love and his pity, redeemed his people, and carried them in the days of old as on eagles' wings, so that none of their proud and spiteful enemies, neither Egyptians nor devils, could touch them.

This was quite a new thing that God did towards this great work of redemption. God never had done anything like it before (Deut. 4:32, 34). This was a great advancement of the work, that had been begun and carried on from the fall of man; a great step taken in Divine Providence towards a preparation for Christ's coming into the world, and working out his great and eternal redemption: for this was the people from whom Christ was to come. And now we may see how that plant flourished which God had planted in Abraham. Though the family of which Christ was to come, had been in a degree separated from the rest of the world before, in the calling of Abraham; yet that separation appeared not to be sufficient. For though by that separation, they were kept, as strangers and sojourners, from being united with other people in the same political societies; yet they remained mixed among them, by which means they had been in danger of wholly losing the true religion, and of being overrun with the idolatry of their neighbours. God now, therefore, by this redemption, separated them as a nation from all others, to subsist by themselves in their own political and ecclesiastical state, without having any concern with the heathen nations, that the church of Christ might be upheld, and might keep the oracles of God; that in them might be kept up those types and prophecies of Christ, and those histories and other divine previous instructions, which were necessary to prepare the way for Christ's coming.

**II.** As this people were separated to be God's peculiar people, so all other people upon the face of the whole earth were wholly rejected and given over to heathenism. This was one thing that God ordered in his providence to prepare the way for Christ's coming, and the great salvation he was to accomplish; for it was only to prepare the way for the more glorious and signal victory and triumph of Christ's power and grace over the wicked and miserable world, and that Christ's salvation of mankind might become the more sensible. This is the account the Scripture itself gives us of the matter, Rom. 11:30, 32. The apostle, speaking to the Gentiles that had formerly been heathens, says, "As ye in times past have not believed God, yet have now obtained mercy through their unbelief; even so have these also now not believed, that through your mercy they also may obtain mercy. For God hath concluded them all in unbelief, that he might have mercy upon all": i.e. It was the will of God, that the whole world, Jews and Gentiles, should be concluded in visible and professed unbelief, that so God's mercy and Christ's salvation towards them all might be visible. For the apostle is not speaking only of that unbelief that is natural to all God's professing people as well as others, but that which appears, and is visible; such as the Jews fell into, when they openly rejected Christ, and ceased to be a professing people. The apostle observes, how that first the Gentiles, even the Gentile nations, were included in at professed unbelief and open opposition to the true religion, before Christ came, to prepare the way for the calling of the Gentiles, which was soon after Christ came, in order that God's mercy might be the more visible to them; and that the Jews were rejected, and apostatized from the visible church, to prepare the way for the calling of the Jews, which shall be in the latter days. So that it may be seen concerning all nations, Jews and Gentiles, that are redeemed by Christ, from being visibly aliens from the commonwealth of Israel, without hope, and without God in the world.

We cannot certainly determine precisely at what time the apostacy of the Gentile nations from the true God, or their being concluded in visible unbelief, became universal. Their falling away was a gradual thing, as we observed before. It was general in Abraham's time, but not universal: for then we find Melchizedek, one of the kings of Canaan, was priest of the most high God. And after this the true religion was kept up for a while among some of the rest of Abraham's posterity, besides the family of Jacob; and also in some of the posterity of Nahor, as we have instances in Job, and his three friends, and Elihu. The land of Uz, where Job lived, was possessed by the posterity of Uz, or Huz, the son of Nahor, Abraham's brother, of whom we read, Gen. 22:21. Bildad the Shuhite was of the offspring of Shuah, Abraham's son by Keturah, Gen. 25:1-2. and Elihu the Buzite, was of Buz the son of Nahor, the brother of Abraham. So the true religion lasted among some other people, besides the Israelites, a while after Abraham. But it did not last long: and it is probable that their total rejection, and giving up to idolatry, was about the time when God separated the children of Israel from Egypt to serve him. For they are often put in mind on that occasion, that God had now separated them to be his peculiar people; or to be distinguished from all other people upon earth, to be his people alone; to be his portion, when others were rejected.

This seems to imply, that God now chose them in such a manner, as was accompanied with a visible rejection of all other nations in the world; that God visibly came, and took up his residence with them, forsaking all other nations. As the first calling of the Gentiles, after Christ came, was accompanied with a rejection of the Jews; so the first calling of the Jews to be God's people, when they left Egypt, was accompanied with a rejection of the Gentiles.

Thus all the nations in the world, except the Israelites, and those who embodied themselves with them, were given up to idolatry; and so continued till Christ came, which was about fifteen hundred years. They were concluded so long a time in unbelief, that there might be a thorough proof of the necessity of a Saviour; that it might appear by so long a trial, past all contradiction, that mankind were utterly insufficient to deliver themselves from that gross darkness and misery, and subjection to the devil; that all the wisdom of the heathen philosophers could not deliver them from their darkness, for the greater glory to Jesus Christ, who, when he came, enlightened and delivered them by his glorious gospel. Herein the wonderful wisdom of God appeared, in thus preparing the way for Christ's redemption. This the Scripture teaches us, 1 Cor. 1:21. "For after that, in the wisdom of God, the world by wisdom knew not God, it pleased God by the foolishness of preaching to save them that believe."

**III.** The next thing done towards the work of redemption, is God's giving the moral law in so awful a manner at mount Sinai. This was another new step taken in this great affair. Deut. 4:33, "Did ever people hear the voice of God speaking out of the midst of the fire, as thou hast heard, and live?" And it was a great thing, whether we consider it as a new exhibition of the covenant of works, or given as a rule of life.

The covenant of works was here exhibited as a schoolmaster to lead to Christ, not only for the use of that nation, under the Old Testament, but for the use of God's church throughout all ages of the world. It is an instrument that the great Redeemer makes use of to convince men of their sin, misery, and helpless state, and of God's awful and tremendous majesty and justice as a lawgiver, in order to make men sensible of the necessity of Christ as a Saviour. This work of redemption, in its saving effect on men's souls, in all its progress, is not carried on without the use of this law delivered at Sinai.

It was given in an awful manner, with a terrible voice, exceedingly loud and awful, so that all the people in the camp trembled; and even Moses himself, though so intimate a friend of God, said, "I exceedingly fear and quake." The voice was accompanied with thunders and lightnings, the mountain burning with fire to the midst of heaven, and the earth itself shaking and trembling. This was done in order to make all sensible how great that authority, power, and justice were, that stood engaged to exact the fulfilment of this law, and to see it fully executed. Here might he understood, how strictly

God would require the fulfilment; and how terrible his wrath would be against every transgressor. Men, being sensible of these things, might thoroughly prove their own hearts, and know how impossible it is for them to obtain salvation by the works of the law, and be assured of their absolute need of a mediator.

If we regard the law given at mount Sinai – not as a covenant of works, but – as a rule of life, it is employed by the Redeemer, from that time to the end of the world, as a directory to his people, to show them the way in which they must walk, as they would go to heaven: for a way of sincere and universal obedience to this law is the narrow way that leads to life.

**IV.** The next thing observable in this period, was God's giving the typical law, those precepts that did not properly belong to the moral law. Not only those laws which are commonly called ceremonial, which prescribe the ceremonies and circumstances of the Jewish worship, and their ecclesiastical state; but also those that were political, for regulating the Jewish commonwealth, commonly called judicial laws, were many of them typical. The giving this typical law was another great thing that God did in this period, tending to build up the glorious structure of redemption. There had been many typical events of providence before, that represented Christ and his redemption, and some typical ordinances, as particularly those two of sacrifices and circumcision: but now, instead of representing the great Redeemer in a few institutions, God enacts a law full of typical representations of good things to come. By these, that nation was directed every year, month, and day, in their religious actions, and in their conduct, in all that appertained to their ecclesiastical and civil state, to something of Christ; one observance exhibiting one doctrine, or one benefit; another, another; so that the whole nation by this law was, as it were, constituted in a typical state. Thus the gospel was abundantly held forth to that nation; so that there is scarce any doctrine of it, but is particularly taught and exhibited by some observance of this law; though it was in shadows, and under a veil, as Moses put a veil on his face when it shone – to this typical law belong all the precepts which relate to building the tabernacle, set up in the wilderness, and all its form, circumstances, and utensils.

**V.** About this time was given to the church the first written word of God. This was another great thing done towards the affair of redemption, a new and glorious advancement of the building; which God has given for the regulation of faith, worship, and practice to the end of the world. This rule grew, and was added to from that time, for many ages, till it was finished, and the canon of Scripture completed by the apostle John. It is not very material, whether the first written word was the Ten Commandments, written on the tables of stone with the finger of God, or the book of Job; and whether the book of Job was written by Moses, as some suppose, or by Elihu, as others. If it was written by Elihu, it must have been before this period; but yet could not be far from it, as appears by considering whose posterity the persons spoken of in it were, together with Job's great age, before it was written.

The written word of God is the main instrument employed by Christ, in order to carry on his work of redemption in all ages. There was a necessity now of the word of God being committed to writing, for a steady rule to God's church. Before this, the church had the word by tradition, either by immediate tradition from eminent men inspired, that were living, or else by tradition from former generations, which might be had with tolerable certainty in ages preceding this, by reason of men's long lives. Noah might converse with Adam, and receive traditions from him; and Noah lived till about Abraham's time: and the sons of Jacob lived a considerable time to deliver the revelations made to Abraham, Isaac, and Jacob, to their posterity in Egypt. But the distance from the beginning of things was become now so great, and the lives of men become so short – being brought down to the present standard about the time of Moses – and God having now separated a nation to be a peculiar people, to be the keepers of the oracles of God; God saw it to be a convenient time now to commit his word to writing, to remain henceforward for a steady rule throughout all ages. And therefore, besides the book of Job, Christ wrote the Ten Commandments on tables of stone, with his own finger. After this, the whole law, as containing the substance of the five books of Moses, was by God's special command committed to writing, which was called "the book of the law," and was laid up in the tabernacle, to be kept there for the use of the church, Deut. 31:24-26.

**VI.** God was pleased now wonderfully to represent the progress of his redeemed church through the world to their eternal inheritance, by the journey of the children of Israel through the wilderness, from Egypt to Canaan. Here all the various steps of the redemption of the church by Christ were represented, from the beginning to its consummation in glory. The state they are redeemed from is represented by Egypt, and their bondage there, which they left. The purchase of their redemption was represented by the sacrifice of the paschal lamb, which was offered up that night in which God slew all the first-born of Egypt. The beginning of the application of the redemption of Christ's church in their conversion, was represented by Israel's going out of Egypt, and passing through the Red Sea in so extraordinary and miraculous a manner. The travel of the church through this evil world, and the various changes through which the church passes, was represented by the journey of the Israelites through the wilderness. The manner of their being conducted by Christ, was represented by the Israelites being led by the pillar of cloud by day, and the pillar of fire by night. The manner of the church's being supported in their progress, supplied with spiritual food, and daily communications from God, was represented by his supplying the children of Israel with manna from heaven, and water out of the rock. The dangers that the saints must meet with in their course through the world, were represented by the fiery flying serpents in the wilderness. The conflicts the church has with her enemies, were represented by their battle with the Amalekites and others. And innumerable other particulars might be mentioned, which were lively images of what the church and saints meet with in all ages of the world. That these things were typical, is manifest from 1 Cor. 10:11, "Now all these things happened unto them for examples, and they were written for our admonition, upon whom the ends of the world are come." Here the apostle is speaking of those very things which we have now mentioned, and he says expressly, that they happened unto them for types; so it is in the original.

**VII.** Another thing here must not be omitted, which was a great and remarkable dispensation of Providence, respecting the whole world of mankind, in this period; viz. the shortening of man's life. It was now brought down from being between nine hundred and a thousand years, to about seventy or eighty. The life of man began to be shortened immediately after the flood. It was brought down the first generation to six hundred years, and the next to between four and five hundred years. So the life of man gradually grew shorter and shorter, till about the time of the great mortality which was in the congregation of Israel, after they had murmured at the report of the spies, and their carcasses fell in the wilderness, whereby all the men of war died. Then the life of man was reduced to its present standard, as Moses observes in that psalm which he wrote on occasion of that mortality: Psalm 90:10, "The days of our years are threescore years and ten; and if by reason of strength they be fourscore years, yet is their strength labour and sorrow; for it is soon cut off, and we fly away."

Man's life being cut so very short, tended to prepare the way for poor, short-lived men, the more joyfully to entertain the glad tidings of everlasting life, brought to light by the gospel; and more readily to embrace a Saviour, that purchases and offers such a blessing. If men's lives were still commonly about nine hundred years, how much less would be the inducement to regard the proffers of a future life; how much greater the temptation to rest in the things of this world, and to neglect any other life but this! This probably contributed greatly to the wickedness of the antediluvians. But now how much greater motives have men to seek redemption, and a better life than this, by the great Redeemer, since the life of man is not one twelfth part of what it used to be, and men now universally die at the age when formerly they used to be but setting out in the world.

**VIII.** The same work was carried on in preserving that people, of whom Christ was to come, from totally perishing in the wilderness, by a constant miracle of forty years' continuance. I observed before how God preserved those of whom the Redeemer was to proceed in a very wonderful manner; as Noah and his family from the flood; Abraham, Isaac, and Jacob, with their families, from the wicked inhabitants of Canaan; and Jacob and his family from perishing by the famine, by Joseph in Egypt. But this preservation of Israel in the wilderness, was on some accounts more remarkable than any of them; for it was by a continual miracle of so long duration. There was, as may be fairly computed, at first two millions worth of souls in that congregation. But if miraculous support had been withheld, they must all have perished, in less than a month's time, so that there would not have been one of them left. But yet this vast multitude subsisted for forty years together, in a dry barren wilderness, without sowing, reaping, or tillage. Their bread was daily rained down to them out of heaven, and they were furnished with water out of a rock; and the same clothes with which they came out of Egypt, lasted all that time. Never was any instance like this, of a nation being so upheld for so long a time together. Thus God upheld his church by a continual miracle, and kept alive that people in whom was the blessing, the great Redeemer of the world.

**IX.** God was pleased, during this time, to give a further revelation of Christ the Redeemer in the predictions of him. Three prophecies deserve particular notice. The first is that of Balaam, Numb. 24:17-19,

> I shall see him, but not now; I shall behold him, but not nigh: there shall come a Star out of Jacob, and a Sceptre shall rise out of Israel, and shall smite the corners of Moab, and destroy all the children of Sheth. And Edom shall be a possession, Seir also shall be a possession for his enemies, and Israel shall do valiantly. Out of Jacob shall come he that shall have dominion, and shall destroy him that remaineth of the city.

This is a plainer prophecy of Christ, especially with regard to his kingly office, than any former one. But we have another, that God gave by Moses, plainer still, especially with regard to his prophetical office, in Deut. 18:18, etc., "I will raise up a prophet from among their brethren, like unto thee, and will put my words in his mouth, and he shall speak unto them all that I command him," etc. This is a plainer prophecy of Christ than any before. All the preceding prophecies were in figurative, mystical language. The first prophecy was so, that the seed of the woman should bruise the serpent's head. The promises made to Abraham, Isaac, and Jacob, that in their seed all the families of the earth should be blessed, were also mystical; and not so particular, because the expression, thy seed, is general, and not plainly limited to any particular person. The prophecy of Jacob in blessing Judah (Gen. 49:8) is in mystical language; and so is that of Balaam, which speaks of Christ under the figurative expression of a star. But this is a plain prophecy, without being veiled at all in any mystical language.

There are several things contained in this prophecy of Christ. Here is his mediatorial office in general (Gen. 49:16). Here it is revealed how he should be a person to stand between them and God, a being of such awful majesty, holiness, and justice, that they could not have come to him, and have intercourse with him immediately, without a mediator to stand between them; because, if they came to such a sin-revenging God immediately, they should die; God would prove a consuming fire to them. And here is a particular revelation of Christ with respect to his prophetical office: "I will raise them up a prophet from among their brethren, like unto thee," etc. And further, it is revealed what kind of a prophet he should be; a prophet like unto Moses, who was the head and leader of all the people, and who, under God, had been their redeemer, to bring them out of the house of bondage. He was their shepherd, by whom God led them through the Red Sea and the wilderness, was an intercessor for them with God, and was both a prophet and a king in the congregation; for Moses had the power of a king among them. It is said of him (Deut. 33:5) that he was king in Jeshurun, was the prophet by whom God built up his church, and delivered his instructions of worship. Thus Christ was to be a prophet like unto Moses; so that this is both the plainest and fullest prophecy of Christ that ever had been from the beginning of the world to this time.

The next prophecy respects the calling of the Gentiles, which should be after Christ's coming (Deut. 32:21). Here is a very plain prophecy of the rejection of the Jews and calling the Gentiles. As they moved God to jealousy, by that which was not God, by casting him off, and taking others, that were no gods, in his place; so God declares that he will move them to jealousy in like manner, by casting them off, and taking others, who had not been his people, in their place. The apostle Paul takes notice of this prophecy, as foretelling the calling of the Gentiles, in Rom. 10:19-20,

> But I say, Did not Israel know? First, Moses saith, I will provoke you to jealousy by them that are no people, and

by a foolish nation I will anger you. But Isaiah is very
bold, and saith, I was found of them that sought me not;
I was made manifest to them that asked not after me.

Thus you see how the light of the gospel, which first
began to dawn and glimmer immediately after the fall,
gradually increases the nearer we come to Christ's time.

**X.** Another thing by which God carried on this work in
this time, was a remarkable pouring out of his Spirit on
the young generation in the wilderness. The generation
that was grown up when they came out of Egypt, from
twenty years old and upward, was a very perverse generation. They were tainted with the idolatry and wickedness of Egypt, and were not weaned from it (Ezek.
20:6-8). Hence they made the golden calf in imitation
of the idolatry of Egypt, that was wont to worship a
bull or an ox; and therefore cattle are called the abom-
ination of the Egyptians, i.e. their idol. With this generation God was exceedingly angry, and swore in his
wrath, that they should not enter into his rest. But the
younger generation, who were under twenty years old
when they came out of Egypt, were not so, Numb.
14:31, "But your little ones, whom ye said should be
a prey, them will I bring in; and they shall know the
land that ye have despised." This was the generation
with whom the covenant was renewed, as we have an
account in Deuteronomy, and that entered into the
land of Canaan. This generation God was pleased to
make a people to his praise, and they were eminent
for piety; as appears by many things said about them;

particularly, Jer. 2:2-3,

> I remember thee, the kindness of thy youth, the love of thine espousals, when thou wentest after me in the wilderness, in a land that was not sown. Israel was holiness to the Lord, and the first-fruits of his increase.

Here the generation that went after God in the wilderness, is spoken of with very high commendations, as eminent for holiness. Their love to God is distinguished like the love of a bride at her espousals, when they followed him through that dreadful wilderness, after they went back from Kadesh-Barnea, Deut. 8:15, "Who led thee through the great and terrible wilderness, wherein were fiery serpents, and scorpions, and drought, where there was no water." Though this generation had a much greater trial, than the generation of their fathers had before they came to Kadesh-Barnea, yet they never murmured against God, as their fathers had done: but their trials had a contrary effect upon them, to awaken, convince, and humble them, and fit them for great mercy. They were awakened by those awful judgments of God inflicted on their fathers, whereby their carcasses fell in the wilderness. God poured out his Spirit with those awakening providences, and their own travel in the wilderness, and the word preached to them by Moses; whereby they were humbled, and at length multitudes of them were savingly converted; as Deut. 8:2-3, "And thou shalt remember the way which the Lord thy God led thee these forty years in the wilderness, to humble thee, and to prove thee, to know what was in thine heart, whether thou wouldst keep his command-

ments, or no. And he humbled thee," etc. And Deut.
8:15, "Who led thee through that great and terrible
wilderness,—that he might humble thee, and that he
might prove thee, to do thee good at thy latter end."
And therefore it is said, Hos. 13:5, "I did know thee
in the wilderness, in the land of great drought." God
allured them, and brought them into that wilderness,
and spake comfortably to them, as it was foretold that
he would do afterwards (Hos. 2:14).

Those terrible judgments that were executed in the
congregation after their turning back from Kadesh-
Barnea, in the matter of Korah, and the matter of Peor,
were chiefly on the old generation, whom God consumed in the wilderness. Those rebellions were chiefly
among the elders of the congregation, who were given
up to their hearts' lust; and they walked in their own
counsels, and God was grieved with their manners forty
years in the wilderness.

That this younger congregation were eminent for
piety, appears by all their history. The former generation
were wicked, and were followed with curses; but this
was holy, and wonderful blessings followed them. God
did great things for them; he fought for them, and gave
them the possession of Canaan. And it is God's manner,
when he hath very great mercies to bestow on a visible
people, first, to fit them for such mercies, and then to
confer them. So it was here: they believed in God, and by
faith overcame Sihon and Og, and the giants of Canaan;
and are commended for cleaving to the Lord: Josh. 23:8,
Joshua says unto them, "Cleave unto the Lord, as ye

have done unto this day." But when Joshua and all that generation were dead, there arose another that knew not the Lord. This pious generation showed a laudable and fervent zeal for God on several occasions; as on occasion of Achan's sin; but especially when they suspected the two tribes and a half had set up an altar in opposition to the altar of burnt-offering. There never was any generation of Israel of which so much good and so little evil is mentioned. It is further observable, that in the time of this generation was the second general circumcision, whereby the reproach of Israel was fully rolled away, and they became pure; and when afterwards they were polluted by Achan, they purged themselves again.

The men of the former generation being dead, and God having sanctified this to himself, he solemnly renewed his covenant with them, as we have a particular account in Deut. 29. We find that such solemn renovations of the covenant commonly accompanied any remarkable pouring out of the Spirit, causing a general reformation: so we find it was in Hezekiah's and Josiah's times. It is questionable whether there ever was a time of so great a flourishing of religion in the Israelitish church, as in that generation; and as, in the Christian church, religion was in its most flourishing circumstances in the day of its espousals, in the apostles' days, so it seems to have been with the Jewish church in the days of its first establishment in the times of Moses and Joshua.

Thus God, at this time, gloriously advanced the work of redemption, both by his word and Spirit. Hereby the work of redemption was promoted, not only as it was in itself a glorious instance of redemption in its application, but as this was what God used for the orderly establishment of the Israelitish church, when it was first settled in the regular observance of God's ordinances in Canaan: even as the pouring out of the Spirit, in the beginning of the Christian church, was a great means for establishing the Christian church in all succeeding ages.

**XI.** The next thing I would observe, was God's bringing the people of Israel by Joshua, and settling them in that land where Christ was to be born, and which was the great type of the heavenly Canaan, which Christ has purchased. Joshua was of Joseph's posterity, and was an eminent type of Christ, and is therefore called the shepherd, the stone of Israel (Gen. 49:24). Being such a type, he bore the name of Christ. Joshua and Jesus are the same name, the one Hebrew, the other Greek: and therefore, in the New Testament, originally written in Greek, Joshua is called Jesus, Acts 7:45, "Which also our fathers brought in with Jesus," i.e. Joshua; Heb. 4:8, "If Jesus had given them rest, he would not have spoken of another day;" i.e. if Joshua had given them rest.

God wonderfully gave his people possession of this land, conquering its former inhabitants, and the mighty giants, as Christ conquered the devil. He first conquered the great kings on the eastern side of Jordan, Sihon king of the Amorites, and Og king of Bashan; and then divided the river Jordan, as before he had done the Red Sea; causing the walls of Jericho to fall down at the sound of the trumpets of the priests. That sound typified

the sound of the gospel by the preaching of gospel min-
isters, the walls of the accursed city Jericho, signifying
the walls of Satan's kingdom. After this he wonderfully
destroyed the mighty host of the Amorites under the five
kings, causing the sun and moon to stand still, to help
the people against their enemies, at the prayer of the
typical Jesus; plainly intimating, that God would make
the whole course of nature to be subservient to the affair
of redemption; and that everything should give place to
the welfare of God's redeemed people.

Thus did Christ show his great love to his elect, that
he would make the course of nature to give place to their
happiness and prosperity; and showed that the sun and
moon, and all things visible and invisible, were theirs
by his purchase. At the same time, Christ fought as the
captain of their host, and cast down great hailstones
upon their enemies, by which more were slain than by
the sword of Israel. And after this Christ gave the people
a mighty victory over a yet greater army in the northern part of the land, gathered together at the waters of
Merom, as the sand of the sea-shore (Josh. 6:4).

Thus God gave the people whence Christ was to
proceed, the land where he was to be born; where he
was to live, preach, and work miracles; to die, and rise
again; and whence he was to ascend into heaven, as the
land which was a great type of heaven.

**XII.** Another thing that God did towards carrying on
this affair, was his actually setting up his stated worship
among the people, as it had been before instituted in

the wilderness. This worship was appointed at mount Sinai; it was to make way for the coming of Christ; and the innumerable ceremonial observances of it were typical of him and his redemption. But there were many parts of their instituted worship that could not be observed in the wilderness, by reason of their unsettled state there. And there were many precepts that respected the land of Canaan, and their places of habitation there, which therefore could not be put in practice, till they came into that land. But now, when this was brought to pass, God set up his tabernacle in the midst of his people, as he had before promised them, Lev. 26:11, "I will set my tabernacle amongst you." The tabernacle was set up at Shiloh (Josh. 18:1) and the priests and the Levites had their offices appointed them, and the cities of refuge, and now the people were in a condition to observe their feasts of the first-fruits, and their feasts of ingathering, and to bring all their tithes and appointed offerings to the Lord; and most parts of God's worship were set up, though there were some things that were not observed till afterwards.

**XIII.** The next thing was God's wonderfully preserving that people, from this time forward, when all the males went up, three times in the year, to the place where God's ark was. The people of Israel were generally surrounded with enemies, who sought all opportunities to destroy them, and dispossess them of their land. Till David's time, there were great numbers in the land of the remains of the Canaanites, and the other former inhabitants of the land, who were bitter enemies to the people of Israel: and these had, three times in the year, a fair opportunity of overrunning their country, and getting possession of their cities, when only the women, and those who were not able to go up, were left behind. And yet they were remarkably preserved throughout all generations at such seasons, agreeably to the promise, Exod. 34:24. "Neither shall any man desire thy land, when thou shalt go up to appear before the Lord thy God thrice in the year." So wonderfully did God order affairs, and influence the hearts of their enemies. They were full of enmity against Israel, desired to dispossess them of their land, and often had so fair an opportunity, that the whole country was left naked and empty of all that could resist them. It would have been only for them to go and take possession; and yet we never read, in all their history, of any of their enemies taking these opportunities against them; which could be no less than a continual miracle, which God, for the preservation of his church, kept up for so many generations. It was surely a wonderful dispensation of Divine Providence to maintain and promote God's great design of redemption.

**XIV.** God's preserving his church and the true religion from being wholly extinct in the frequent apostacies of the Israelites in the time of the judges. How prone was that people to forsake the true God, who had done such wonderful things for them, and to fall into idolatry! And how did the land, from time to time, seem to be almost overrun with it! But yet God never suffered his true worship to be totally rooted out: his tabernacle stood, the ark was preserved, the book of the law was kept from being destroyed, God's priesthood was upheld, and he still had a church among the people. Time after time, when religion seemed to be almost gone, then God granted a revival, and sent some angel, or raised up some eminent person, to be an instrument of their reformation.

**XV.** God's preserving that nation from being destroyed, although they were so often subdued and brought under the dominion of their enemies. It was a wonder, not only that the true religion was not wholly rooted out, and so the church destroyed that way; but also that the very nation in which that church was, was not utterly destroyed; they were so often brought under the power of their enemies. One while they were subdued by Chushan-rishathaim king of Mesopotamia, another while they were brought under the Moabites; now they were sold into the hand of Jabin king of Canaan; then they were under the dominion of the Midianites; now they were sorely distressed by the children of Ammon; and then by the Philistines. But yet God, in all these dangers, preserved them, and kept them from being wholly overthrown. From time to time, when it was come to extremity, and God saw that they were upon the very brink of ruin, then he raised up a deliverer, agreeable to Deut. 32:36, "For the Lord shall judge his people, and repent himself for his servants; when he seeth their power is gone, and there is none shut up or left." – Those remarkable dispensations of Providence are very elegantly set forth by the psalmist, Psalm

106:34, etc. – these deliverers were all types of Christ, the great redeemer and deliverer of his church; and some of them very remarkably so; as, Barak, Jephthah, Gideon, and Samson, in very many particulars; and above all in the acts of Samson, as might be shown, were it not that this would take up too much time.

**XVI.** It is observable, that when Christ appeared to manage the affairs of his church in this period, he often appeared in the form of that nature which he took upon him in his incarnation. So he seems to have appeared repeatedly to Moses, and particularly at that time when God spake to him face to face, as a man speaketh to his friend, and he beheld the similitude of the Lord, (Numb. 12:8) after he had besought him to show him his glory; which was the most remarkable vision that ever he had of Christ. There was a twofold discovery that Moses had of Christ: one was spiritual, made to his mind, by the word that was proclaimed, Exod. 34:6-7,

> The Lord, the Lord God, merciful and gracious, long-suffering, and abundant in goodness and truth, keeping mercy for thousands, forgiving iniquity and transgression and sin, and that will by no means clear the guilty; visiting the iniquity of the fathers upon the children, and upon the children's children, unto the third and to the fourth generation,

Another was external; which was that which Moses saw, when Christ passed by, and put him in a cleft of the rock. What he saw was doubtless a glorious human

form, in which Christ appeared to him, and in all likelihood the form of his glorified human nature, in which
he should afterwards appear. He saw not his face; for it
is not to be supposed that any man could subsist under
a sight of the glory of Christ's human nature as it now
appears.

So it was a human form in which Christ appeared
to the seventy elders, of which we have an account,
Exod. 24: 9-11.

> Then went up Moses and Aaron, Nadab and Abihu, and
> seventy of the elders of Israel. And they saw the God of
> Israel: and there was under his feet, as it were a paved
> work of sapphire-stone, and as it were the body of heaven
> in his clearness. And upon the nobles of the children of
> Israel he laid not his hand: also they saw God, and did
> eat and drink.

So Christ appeared afterwards to Joshua in the form of
the human nature, Josh. 5: 13-14.

> And it came to pass when Joshua was by Jericho, he lift
> up his eyes, and looked, and behold, there stood a man
> over against him, with his sword drawn in his hand: and
> Joshua went unto him, and said unto him, Art thou for
> us, or for our adversaries? And he said, Nay, but as captain
> of the host of the Lord am I now come.

And so he appeared to Gideon, Judg. 6:11, &c. and so
also to Manoah, Judg. 13:17-21. Here Christ appeared
to Manoah in a representation both of his incarnation
and death; of his incarnation, in that he appeared in
a human form; and of his death and sufferings, repre-

sented by the sacrifice of a kid, and by his ascending up in the flame of the sacrifice; intimating, that it was he that was the great sacrifice, that must be offered up to God for a sweet savour, in the fire of his wrath, as that kid was burned and ascended up in the flame. Thus Christ appeared, time after time, in the form of that nature he was afterwards to assume; because he now appeared on the same design and to carry on the same work.

**XVII.** Another thing I would mention, done in this period towards the work of redemption, is the beginning of a succession of prophets, and erecting a school of the prophets, in Samuel's time. There was something of this spirit of prophecy in Israel after Moses, before Samuel. Joshua and many of the judges had a degree of it. Deborah was a prophetess; and some of the high-priests were inspired with this spirit; particularly Eli. That space of time was not wholly without instances of those that were set apart of God especially to this office, and so were called prophets. We read in Judg. 6:8. "The Lord sent a prophet unto the children of Israel, which said unto them," &c. Such an one he seems to have been of whom we read, 1 Sam. 2:27. "And there came a man of God to Eli." &c

But there was no such order of men upheld in Israel, for any constancy, before Samuel; the want of it is taken notice of in 1 Sam. 3:1. "And the word of the Lord was precious in those days; there was no open vision." But in Samuel there was begun succession of prophets, maintained continually from that time, at least with very little interruption, till the spirit of prophecy ceased, about Malachi's time: and therefore Samuel is spoken of in the New Testament as the beginning of this succession of prophets, Acts 3:24. "And all the prophets from Samuel, and those that follow after, as many as have spoken, have foretold of these days." After Samuel was Nathan, and Gad, Iddo, and Heman, Asaph, and others. And afterwards, in the latter end of Solomon's reign, we read of Ahijah; and in Jeroboam and Rehoboam's time we read of prophets; and so continually one prophet succeeded another till the captivity. In the writings of those prophets who are inserted in the canon of Scripture, we read of prophets as being a constant order of men upheld in the land. And even during the captivity there were prophets still, as Ezekiel and Daniel; and after the captivity, as Zechariah, Haggai, and Malachi.

And because God intended a constant succession of prophets from Samuel's time, therefore in his time was begun a school of the prophets; that is, a school of young men, trained up under some great prophet, who was their master and teacher in the study of divine things, and the practice of holiness, to fit them for this office as God should call them to it. Those young men were called the sons of the prophets; and oftentimes they are termed prophets. These at first were under the tuition of Samuel. Thus we read of Samuel's being appointed over them, 1 Sam. 19: 20. "And when they saw the company of the prophets prophesying, and Samuel standing as appointed over them." The company of prophets of whom we read 1 Sam. 5:5. were the same. Afterwards we read of their being under Elijah. Elisha was one of these sons; but he desired to have a double portion of his spirit, as his successor, as the eldest son was wont to have a double portion of the estate of his father; and therefore the sons of the prophets, when they perceived that the spirit of Elijah rested on Elisha, submitted themselves to him, and owned him for their master, as they had done Elijah before him, 2 Kings 2:15. "And when the sons of the prophets which were to view at Jericho, saw him, they said, The spirit of Elijah doth rest on Elisha. And they bowed themselves to the ground before him." Elisha being their master, or teacher, he had the care of them; as you may see, 2 Kings 4:38. "And Elisha came unto Gilgal, and there was a dearth in the land, and the sons of the prophets were sitting before him: and he said unto his servant, Set on the great pot, and seethe pottage for the sons of the prophets." In Elijah's and Elisha's time, there were several places where there resided companies of these sons of the prophets; as at Bethel, at Jericho, and at Gilgal, unless that at Gilgal and Jericho were the same: and possibly that which is called the college, where the prophetess Huldah resided, was another at Jerusalem; see 2 Kings 22:14. It is there said of Huldah the prophetess, that she dwelt in Jerusalem, in the college. They had houses built, where they used to dwell together; and therefore those at Jericho being multiplied, and finding their house too little for them, desired leave of their master and teacher Elisha, that they might go and hew timber to build a bigger; as you may see, 2 Kings 6:1-2. At some times there were numbers of these sons of the prophets in Israel; for when Jezebel cut off the prophets of the Lord, it is said, that Obadiah took a hundred of them, and hid them by fifty in a cave, 1 Kings 18:4.

These schools of the prophets being set up by Samuel, and afterwards kept up by such as Elijah and Elisha, must be of divine appointment; and accordingly we find, that those sons of the prophets were often favored with a degree of inspiration, while they continued under tuition: and God commonly when he called any prophet to the constant exercise of the prophetical office, and to some extraordinary service, took them out of these schools; though not universally. Hence the prophet Amos, speaking of his being called to the prophetical office, says, that he had not been educated in the schools of the prophets, and was not one of the sons of the prophets, Amos 7:14- 15. But Amos taking notice of it as remarkable, that he should be so called, shows that it was God's ordinary manner to take his prophets out of these schools; for therein he did but blessed his own institution.

Now this remarkable dispensation of providence—God beginning a constant succession of prophets in Samuel's time, which was to last for many ages; and to that end establishing a school of the prophets under Samuel, thenceforward to be continued in Israel—was a step that God took in the great affair of redemption. For the main business of this succession of prophets was, to foreshow Christ, and the glorious redemption he was to accomplish, and so to prepare the way for his coming; as appears by that fore-mentioned place, Acts 3:24. and Acts 10: 43. "To him give all the prophets witness;" and Acts 3:18. "But those things which God before had showed by the mouth of all his prophets, that Christ should suffer, he hath so fulfilled."

The Old-Testament church was not wholly without light, but had not the light of the sun directly, only as reflected. Now these prophets were the luminaries that reflected the light of the sun; and accordingly they spoke abundantly of Jesus Christ, as appears by what we have of their prophecies in writing. And they made it very much their business, when they studied in their schools or colleges, and elsewhere, to search out the work of redemption; agreeable to what the apostle Peter says of them, 1 Pet. 1:10-11.

> Of which salvation the prophets have inquired, and searched diligently, who prophesied of the grace that should come unto you; searching what, or what manner of time the Spirit of Christ that was in them did signify, when it testified beforehand the sufferings of Christ, and the glory that should follow.

We are told, that the church of the Redeemer is built on the foundation of the prophets and apostles, the Redeemer himself being the chief corner-stone, Eph. 2:20.

This was the first thing of the nature that ever was done in the world; and it was a great thing that God did towards further advancing this great building of redemption. There had been before occasional prophecies of

Christ, as was shown; but now the time drawing nearer when the Redeemer should come, it pleased God to appoint a certain order of men, in constant succession, whose main business it should be, to point out Christ and his redemption, and as his forerunners to prepare the way for his coming; and God established schools, wherein multitudes were instructed and trained up to that end, Rev. 19:10. "I am thy fellow-servant, and of thy brethren that have the testimony of Jesus; for the testimony of Jesus is the spirit of prophecy."

## 1.5 PART V
### 6.0 From David to the Babylonian Captivity

I COME NOW to the fifth period of the times of the Old Testament, beginning with David, and extending to the Babylonish captivity; and would now proceed to show how the work of redemption was therein carried on.—And here,

**I.** The first thing to be noticed is God's anointing that person who was to be the ancestor of Christ, to be king over his people. The dispensations of Providence through the last period, respect the people whence Christ was to proceed; but now the Scripture leads us to consider God's providence towards that particular person whence Christ was to descend, viz. David. It pleased God at this time remarkably to select out this person, from all the thousands of Israel, and to put a most honourable mark of distinction upon him, by anointing him to be king over his people. It was only God that could find him out. His father's house is spoken of as being little in Israel, and he was the youngest of all the sons of his father, and was least expected by Samuel to be the man whom God had chosen. God had before, in the former ages of the world, remarkably distinguished the persons from whom Christ was to come; as Seth, and Noah, and Abraham, and Isaac, and Jacob. But the last that we have any account of God's marking out in any notable manner, the very person of whom Christ was to come, was in Jacob's blessing, his son Judah; unless we reckon Nahshon's advancement in the wilderness to be the head of the tribe of Judah. But this distinction of the person of whom Christ was to come, in David, was very honourable; for it was God's anointing him to be king over his people. And there was something further denoted by David's anointing, than was in the anointing of Saul. God anointed Saul to be king personally; but God intended something further by sending Samuel to anoint David, viz. to establish the crown of Israel in him and his family, as long as Israel continued to be a kingdom: and not only so, but what was infinitely more still, establishing the crown of his universal church, his spiritual Israel, in his seed, to the end of the world, and through eternity.

This was a great dispensation of God, and a great step taken towards a further advancing of the work of redemption, according as the time drew near wherein Christ was to come. David, as he was the ancestor of Christ, so he was the greatest personal type of Christ of all under the Old Testament. The types of Christ were of three sorts; instituted, providential, and personal. The ordinance of sacrificing was the greatest of the instituted types; the redemption out of Egypt was the greatest of the providential; and David the greatest of the personal ones. Hence Christ is often called David in the prophecies of Scripture; as Ezek. 34: 23-24. "And I will set up one shepherd over them, and he shall feed them, even my servant David;—My servant David a prince among them;" and so in many other places. He is very often spoken of as the seed and the son of David.

David being the ancestor and great type of Christ, his being solemnly anointed by God to be king over his people, that the kingdom of his church might be continued in his family for ever, may in some respects be looked on as an anointing of Christ himself. Christ was as it were anointed in him; and therefore Christ's anointing and David's anointing are spoken of under one scripture, Psalm 89:20, "I have found David my servant; with my holy oil have I anointed him."

And David's throne and Christ's are spoken of as one: Luke 1:32, "And the Lord shall give him the throne of his father David." Acts 2:30, "David—knowing that God had sworn with an oath to him, that of the fruit of his loins, according to the flesh, he would raise up Christ to sit on his throne."

Thus God beginning the kingdom of his church in the house of David, was, as it were, a new establishing of the kingdom of Christ; the beginning of it in a state of such visibility as it thenceforward continued in. It was planting the root, whence that branch of righteousness was afterwards to spring up, the everlasting king of his church; and therefore this everlasting king is called the branch from the stem of Jesse. Isa. 11:1, "And there shall come forth a rod out of the stem of Jesse, and a branch shall grow out of his roots." Jer. 23:5, "Behold, the days come, saith the Lord, that I will raise up unto David a righteous branch, and a king shall reign and prosper." So Jer. 33:15. "In those days, and at that time, I will cause the branch of righteousness to grow up unto David, and he shall execute judgment and righteousness in the land." So Christ, in the New Testament, is called the root and offspring of David, Rev.22:16.

It is observable, that God anointed David after Saul to reign in his room. He took away the crown from him and his family, who was higher in stature than any of his people, and was in their eyes fittest to bear rule; to give it to David, who was low of stature, and in comparison of despicable appearance. So God was pleased to show how Christ, who appeared despicable, without form or comeliness, and was despised and rejected of men, should take the kingdom from the great ones of the earth. And also it is observable, that David was the youngest of Jesse's sons, as Jacob the younger brother supplanted Esau, and got the birthright and blessing from him; and as Pharez, brother of Christ's ancestor, supplanted Zarah in the birth; and as Isaac, another of the ancestors of Christ, cast out his elder brother Ishmael: thus was that frequent saying of Christ fulfilled," The last shall be first, and the first last."

**II.** The next thing I would observe, is God's preserving David's life, by a series of wonderful providences, till Saul's death. I before took notice of the wonderful preservation of other particular persons who were the ancestors of Christ; as Noah, Abraham, Isaac, Jacob; and have observed how, in their preservation, the work of redemption itself may be looked upon as preserved from being defeated, and the whole church, which is redeemed through him, from being overthrown. But the preservation of David was no less remarkable than that of any others already noticed. How often was there but a step between him and death. The first instance of it we have in his encountering a lion and a bear, when they had caught a lamb out of his flock, which, without miraculous assistance, could at once have rent this young stripling in pieces, as easily as they could the lamb that he delivered from them. So the root and offspring of David was preserved from the roaring lion that goes about seeking whom he may devour, and conquered him, and rescued the souls of men, that were as lambs in the mouth of this lion. Another remarkable instance was, in preserving him from that mighty giant Goliath, who was strong enough to have torn him to pieces, and given his flesh to the beasts of the field, and to the fowls of the air, as he threatened. But God preserved him, and gave him the victory over Goliath, so that he cut off his head with his own sword, and thus was made the deliverer of Israel. So Christ slew the spiritual Goliath with his own weapon, the cross, and delivered his represented people. And how remarkably did God preserve David from being slain by Saul, when he first sought his life! He gave him his daughter to be a snare to him, that the hand of the Philistines might be upon him, requiring of him a hundred foreskins of the Philistines, that so his life might be exposed to them. The same divine care was evident in preserving him afterwards, when Saul spake to Jonathan, and to all his servants, to kill David; and in inclining Jonathan, instead of his killing him, as his father commanded, to love him as his own soul, and to be a great instrument of his preservation, even so as to expose his own life to preserve David; though one would have thought that none would have been more willing to have David killed than Jonathan, seeing that he was competitor with him for the crown. Again, Saul threw a javelin at him, to smite him even to the wall; and sent messengers to his house, to watch, and to kill him, when Michal, Saul's daughter, let him down through a window. He afterwards sent messengers once and again, to Naioth in Ramah, to take him, and they were remarkably prevented by miraculous impressions of the Spirit of God; and afterwards, when Saul, being resolute in the affair, went himself, he also was among the prophets. How wonderfully was David's life preserved at Gath among the Philistines, when he went to Achish the king of Gath, and was there in the hands of the Philistines, who, one would have thought, would have dispatched him at once, he having so much provoked them by his exploits against them. He was again wonderfully preserved at Keilah, when he had entered into a fenced town, where Saul thought he was sure of him. And how wonderfully was he preserved from Saul, when he pursued and hunted him in the mountains! How remarkably did God deliver him in the wilderness of Maon, when Saul and his army were compassing David about! How was he delivered in the cave of Engedi, when, instead of Saul's killing David, God delivered Saul into his hands in the cave! David cut off his skirt, and might as easily have cut off his head. He was delivered in like manner in the wilderness of Ziph; and afterwards preserved in the land of the Philistines, though David had fought against the Philistines, and conquered them at Keilah, since he was last among them. This, one would think, would have been sufficient warning to them not to trust him, or let him escape a second time, if ever they had him in their hands again; but yet now, when they had a second opportunity, God wonderfully turned their hearts to befriend and protect, instead of destroying him.

Thus was the precious seed that virtually contained the Redeemer, and all the blessings of his redemption, wonderfully preserved, when hell and earth were conspired to destroy it. How often does David himself take notice of this, with praise and admiration, in the book of Psalms!

**III.** About this time, the written word of God, or the canon of Scripture, was augmented by Samuel. I have before observed, that the canon of Scripture was begun and the first written rule of faith and manners was given to the church, about the time of Moses. Joshua probably enlarged it, and wrote the last chapter of

Deuteronomy, and most of the book of Joshua. Others think that Joshua, Judges, Ruth, and part of the first book of Samuel, were written by Samuel. However that was, of this we have good evidence, that Samuel made an addition to the canon of Scripture; for Samuel is manifestly mentioned in the New Testament, as one of the prophets whose writings we have in Scripture, Acts 3:24. "Yea and all the prophets from Samuel, and those that follow after, as many as have spoken, have likewise foretold of these days." By that expression, "as many as have spoken," is meant, as many as have spoken by writing.

And the way that Samuel spoke of these times of Christ and the gospel, was by giving the history of those things that typified, and pointed to them, particularly what he wrote concerning David. The Spirit of God moved him to commit those things to writing, chiefly because they pointed to Christ, and the times of the gospel; and, as was said before, this was the main business of all that succession of prophets that began in Samuel. That Samuel added to the canon of the Scriptures seems further to appear from 1 Chron. 39:29. "Now the acts of David the king, first and last, behold they are written in the book of Samuel the seer."

Whether the book of Joshua was written by Samuel or not, yet it is the general opinion of divines, that the books of Judges and Ruth, and part of the first book of Samuel, were penned by him. The book of Ruth was penned for this reason, that though it seemed to treat of private affairs, yet the persons chiefly spoken of were of the family whence David and Christ proceeded, and so pointed to what the apostle Peter observed of Samuel and the other prophets, in the third chapter of Acts. These additions to the canon of the Scripture, the great and main instrument of the application of redemption, are to be considered as a further continuation of that work, and an addition made to that great building.

**IV.** Another thing God did towards this work, at that time, was his inspiring David to show forth Christ and his redemption, in divine songs, which should be for the use of the church, in public worship, throughout all ages. David was himself endued with the spirit of prophecy. He is called a prophet, Acts 2:29-30. "Let me freely speak to you of the patriarch David, that he is both dead and buried, and his sepulchre is with us unto this day; therefore being a prophet, and knowing that God had sworn with an oath," &c. So that herein he was a type of Christ, that he was both a prophet and a king.

The oil that was used in anointing David was a type of the Spirit of God; and the type and the ante-type were given both together; as we are told, 1 Sam. 16:13. "Then Samuel took the horn of oil, and anointed him in the midst of his brethren; and the Spirit of the Lord came upon David from that day forward:" and it is probable, that it now came upon him in its prophetical influences. One way that this Spirit influenced him was by inspiring him to show forth Christ, and the glorious things of his redemption, in divine songs, sweetly expressing the breathings of a pious soul, full of admiration of the glorious things of the Redeemer, inflamed with divine love and elevated praise; and therefore he is called the sweet psalmist of Israel, 2 Sam. 23:1. The main subjects of these songs were the glorious things of the gospel; as is evident by the interpretation that is often put upon them, and the use that is made of them in the New Testament: for there is no one book of the Old Testament that is so often quoted in the New, as the book of Psalms. Joyfully did this holy man sing of those great things of Christ's redemption, that had been the hope and expectation of God's church and people from the beginning; and joyfully did others follow him in it, as Asaph, Heman, Ethan, and others; for the book of Psalms was not all penned by David, though the greater part of it was. Hereby the canon of the Scripture was further enlarged by an excellent portion of divine writ.

This was a great advancement that God made in this building; and the light of the gospel, which had been gradually growing, was exceedingly increased by it: for whereas before there was but here and there a prophecy given of Christ in a great many ages, here Christ is spoken of by his ancestor David abundantly, in multitudes of songs, speaking of his incarnation, life, death, resurrection, ascension into heaven, his satisfaction, intercession; his prophetical, kingly, and priestly office; his glorious benefits in this life and that which is to come; his union with the church, and the blessedness of the church in him; the calling of the Gentiles, the future glory of the church near the end of the world, and Christ's coming to the final judgment. All these things, and many more, concerning Christ and his redemption, are abundantly spoken of in the book of Psalms.

This was also a glorious advancement of the affair of redemption, as God hereby gave his church a book of divine songs for their use in that part of their public worship, viz. singing his praises, throughout all ages to the end of the world. It is manifest the book of Psalms was given of God for this end. It was used in the church of Israel by God's appointment: this is manifest by the title of many of the Psalms, in which they are inscribed to the chief musician, i.e. to the man that was appointed to be the leader of divine songs in the temple, in the public worship of Israel. So David is called the sweet psalmist of Israel, because he penned psalms for the use of the church of Israel; and accordingly we have an account that they were actually made use of in the church of Israel for that end, even ages after David was dead; as 2 Chron. 29:30. "Moreover, Hezekiah the king, and the princes, commanded the Levites to sing praises unto the Lord, with the words of David, and of Asaph the seer." And we find that the same are appointed in the New Testament to be made use of in the Christian church, in their worship: Eph. 5:19. "Speaking to yourselves in psalms, hymns, and spiritual songs." Col. 3:16. "Admonishing one another in psalms, hymns, and spiritual songs." So they have been, and will, to the end of the world, be made use of in the church to celebrate the praises of God. The people of God were wont sometimes to worship God by singing songs to his praise before; as they did at the Red sea; and they had Moses's prophetical song, in the 32d chapter of Deuteronomy, committed to them for that end; and Deborah, Barak, and Hannah sung praises to God: but now first did God commit to his church a book of divine songs for their constant use.

V. The next thing I would notice, is God's actually exalting David to the throne of Israel, notwithstanding all the opposition made to it. God was determined to do it, and he made every thing give place that stood in its way. He removed Saul and his sons out of the way; and first set David over the tribe of Judah; then, having removed Ishbosheth, set him over all Israel. Thus did God fulfil his word to David. He took him from the sheep-cote, and made him king over his people Israel, Psalm 78:70, 71. And now the throne of Israel was established in that family in which it was to continue for ever.

VI. Now first it was that God proceeded to choose a particular city out of all the tribes of Israel to place his name. There is several times mention made in the law of Moses, of the children of Israel bringing their oblations to the place which God should choose; as Deut. 12: 5-7. and other places; but God had never proceeded to do it till now. The tabernacle and ark were never fixed, but sometimes in one place, and sometimes in another; but now God proceeded to choose Jerusalem. The city of Jerusalem was never thoroughly conquered, or taken out of the hands of the Jebusites, till David's time. It is said in Joshua 15:63. "As for the Jebusites, the inhabitants of Jerusalem, the children of Judah could not drive them out: but the Jebusites dwell with the children of Judah at Jerusalem unto this day." But now David wholly subdued it, as we have an account in 2 Sam. 5. And now God proceeded to choose that city to place his name there, as appears by David's bringing up the ark thither soon after; and therefore this is mentioned afterwards as the first time God proceeded to choose a city to that end. 2 Chron. 6:5-6, 12: 13. Afterwards God proceeded to show David the very place where he would have his temple built, viz. in the threshing-floor of Araunah the Jebusite.

This city of Jerusalem is therefore called the holy city; and it was the greatest type of the church of Christ in all the Old Testament. It was redeemed by David, the captain of the hosts of Israel, out of the hands of the Jebusites, to be God's city, the holy place of his rest for ever, where he would dwell. So Christ, the Captain of his people's salvation, redeems his church out of the hands of devils, to be his holy and beloved city. And therefore how often does the Scripture, when speaking of Christ's redemption of his church, call it by the names of Zion and Jerusalem! This was the city that God had appointed to be the place of the first gathering and erecting of the Christian church after Christ s resurrection, of that remarkable effusion of the Spirit of God on the apostles and primitive Christians, and the place whence the gospel was to sound forth into all the world; the place of the first Christian church, that was to be, as it were, the mother of all other churches through the world; agreeable to that prophecy, Isa. 2:3-4. "Out of Zion shall go forth the law, and the word of the Lord from Jerusalem: and he shall judge among the nations, and shall rebuke many people," &c. Thus God chose mount Zion whence the gospel was to be sounded forth, as the law had been from mount Sinai.

**VII.** The next thing to be observed here, is God's solemnly renewing the covenant of grace with David, and promising that the Messiah should be of his seed. We have an account of it in the 7th chapter of the second book of Samuel. It was done on occasion of the thoughts David entertained of building God a house. On this occasion God sends Nathan the prophet to him, with the glorious promises of the covenant of grace. It is especially contained in these words, 2 Sam 7:16. "And thy house and thy kingdom shall be established for ever before thee; thy throne shall be established for ever." Which promise has respect to Christ, the seed of David, and is fulfilled in him only: for the kingdom of David has long since ceased, any otherwise than as it is upheld in Christ.

That this covenant, now established with David by Nathan the prophet, was the covenant of grace, is evident by the plain testimony of Scripture, Isa. 1:1-3. There we have Christ inviting sinners to come to the waters, &c. And in "Isa. 1:3. he says, "Incline your ear, and come unto me; hear and your souls shall live; and I will make with you an everlasting covenant, even the sure mercies of David." Here Christ offers to poor sinners, if they will come to him, to give them an interest in the same everlasting covenant that he had made with David, conveying to them the same sure mercies. But what is that covenant, in which sinners obtain an interest when they come to Christ, but the covenant of grace?

This was the fifth solemn establishment of the covenant of grace with the church after the fall. The covenant of grace was revealed and established all along. But there had been particular seasons, wherein God had in a very solemn manner renewed this covenant with his church, giving forth a new edition and establishment of it, revealing it in a new manner. The first was with Adam; the second with Noah; the third with the patriarchs, Abraham, Isaac, and Jacob; the fourth was in the wilderness by Moses; and now the fifth is made to David.

This establishment of the covenant of grace, David always esteemed the greatest smile of God upon him, the greatest honour put upon him; he prized it, and rejoiced in it above all the other blessings of his reign. You may see how joyfully and thankfully he received it, when Nathan came to him with the glorious message, 2 Sam. 7:18., &c. And so David, in his last words, declares this to be all his salvation, and all his desire; "He hath made with me an everlasting covenant, ordered in all things and sure: for this is all my salvation, and all my desire."

**VIII.** It was by David that God first gave his people Israel the possession of the whole promised land. I have before shown, how God giving possession of the promised land belonged to the covenant of grace. This was done in a great measure by Joshua, but not fully. Joshua did not wholly subdue that part of the promised land that was strictly called the land of Canaan, and that was divided by lot to the several tribes; but there were great numbers of the old inhabitants left unsubdued, as we read in the books of Joshua and Judges; and there were many left to prove Israel, and to be as thorns in their sides. There were the Jebusites in Jerusalem, and many of the Canaanites, and the whole nation of the Philistines, who all dwelt in that part of the land that was divided by lot, and chiefly in that which belonged to the tribes of Judah and Ephraim.

And thus these remains of the old inhabitants of Canaan continued unsubdued till David's time; but he wholly subdued them all. Which is agreeable to what St. Stephen observes, Acts 7:45. "Which also our fathers brought in with Jesus (i.e. Joshua) into the possession of the Gentiles, whom God drove out before the face of our fathers, unto the days of David." They were till the days of David in driving them out, before they had wholly subdued them. But David entirely brought them under. He subdued the Jebusite, the whole nation of the Philistines, and all the rest of the remains of the seven nations of Canaan; 1 Chron. 18:1. "Now after this it came to pass, that David smote the Philistines, and subdued them, and took Gath and her towns out of the hands of the Philistines."

After this, all the remains of the former inhabitants of Canaan were made bond-servants to the Israelites. The posterity of the Gibeonites became servants before, hewers of wood, and drawers of water, for the house of God. But Solomon, David's son and successor, put

184 | A CELEBRATION OF FAITH: JONATHAN EDWARDS

all the other remains of the seven nations of Canaan to bond-service; at least made them pay a tribute of bond-service, 1 Kings 9:20-22. And hence we read of the children of Solomon's servants, after the return from the Babylonish captivity, Ezra 2:55. and Neh. 11:3. They were the children or posterity of the seven nations of Canaan, that Solomon had subjected to bond-service.

Thus David subdued the whole land of Canaan, strictly so called. But then that was not one half, nor quarter, of the land God had promised to their fathers. The land often promised to their fathers, included all the countries from the river of Egypt to the river Euphrates. These were the bounds of the land promised to Abraham, Gen. 15:19. "In that same day the Lord made a covenant with Abram, saying. Unto thy seed have I given this land, from the river of Egypt, unto the great river, the river Euphrates." So again God promised at mount Sinai, Exod. 23:31.

"And I will set thy bounds from the Red sea even unto the sea of the Philistines, and from the desert unto the river: for I will deliver the inhabitants of the land into your hand; and thou shalt drive them out before thee." So again, Deut. 11:24. "Every place whereon the soles of your feet shall tread, shall be yours: from the wilderness, and Lebanon, from the river, the river Euphrates, even unto the uttermost sea, shall your coast be." Again, the same promise is made to Joshua: Josh. 1:3-4.

> Every place that the sole of your feet shall tread upon, have I given unto you, as I said unto Moses; from the

wilderness and this Lebanon, even unto the great river, the river Euphrates, all the land of the Hittites, and unto the great sea, towards the going down of the sun, shall be your coast.

But the land of which Joshua gave the people possession, was but a little part of this land. And the people never had possession of it, till now when God gave it them by David.

This large country did not only include that Canaan which was divided by lot to those who came in with Joshua, but the land of the Moabites and Ammonites, the land of the Amalekites, and the rest of the Edomites, and the country of Zobah. All these nations were subdued and brought under the children of Israel by David. And he put garrisons in the several countries, and they became David's servants, as we have a particular account in the 8th chapter of 2d Samuel: and David extended their border to the river Euphrates, as was promised; see the 3d verse: 2 Sam. 8:3. "And David smote also Hadadezer the son of Rehob, king of Zobah, as he went to recover his border at the river Euphrates." And accordingly we read, that Solomon his son reigned over all the region on this side the river, 1 Kings 4:24. "For he had dominion over all the region on this side the river, from Tiphsah even unto Azzah, over all the kings on this side the river." This Artaxerxes king of Persia takes notice of long after: Ezra 4:20. "There have been mighty kings also over Jerusalem, which have ruled over all countries beyond the river; and toll, tribute, and custom was paid unto them."

So that Joshua, that eminent type of Christ, did but begin the work of giving Israel the possession of the promised land; but left it to be finished by that much greater type and ancestor of Christ, even David, who subdued far more of that land than ever Joshua had done. And in this extent of his and Solomon's dominion was some resemblance of the great extent of Christ's kingdom; which is set forth by this very thing, Psalm 22:8. "He shall have dominion also from sea to sea, and from the river unto the ends of the earth." See also 1 Kings 8:56.

**IX.** God by David perfected the Jewish worship, and added to it several new institutions. The law was given by Moses, but yet all the institutions of the Jewish worship were not given by Moses; some were added by divine direction. So this greatest of all personal types of Christ did not only perfect Joshua's work, in giving Israel the possession of the promised land, but he also finished Moses's work, in perfecting the instituted worship of Israel. Thus there must be a number of typical prophets, priests, and princes, to complete one figure or shadow of Christ the antetype, he being the substance of all the types and shadows. Of so much more glory was Christ accounted worthy, than Moses, Joshua, David, and Solomon, and all the great prophets, priests, and princes, judges, and saviours of the Old Testament put together.

The ordinances of David are mentioned as of parallel validity with those of Moses, 2 Chron. 23:18. "Also

Jehoiada appointed the offices of the house of the Lord by the hand of the priests the Levites, whom David had distributed in the house of the Lord, to offer the burnt-offerings of the Lord, as it is written in the law of Moses, with rejoicing and with singing, as it was ordained by David."

The worship of Israel was perfected by David, by the addition he made to the ceremonial law, (1 Chron. 33. &c.) consisting in the several orders and courses into which the Levites were divided, and the work and business to which he appointed them, different from what Moses had appointed them to; and also in the divisions of the priests, the sons of Aaron, into four and twenty courses, assigning to every course their business in the house of the Lord, and their particular stated times of attendance there. He also appointed some of the Levites to a new office, that of singers, particularly ordering and regulating them in that office, ( 1 Chron. 25. ) Others of the Levites he appointed by law to the several services of porters, treasurers, officers, and judges: and these ordinances of David were kept up thenceforth in the church of Israel, as long as the Jewish church lasted. Thus we find the several orders of priests, and the Levites, the porters, and singers, after the captivity. And we find the courses of the priests appointed by David still continuing in the New Testament; Zacharias the father of John the Baptist was a priest of the course of Abia; which is the same with the course of Abijah appointed by David, 1 Chron. 24:10.

Thus David as well as Moses was made like to Christ the Son of David, in this respect, that by him God gave, in a manner, a new ecclesiastical establishment, and new institutions of worship. David did not only add to the institutions of Moses, but by those additions he abolished some of the old institutions that had been in force till that time; particularly those laws which appointed the business of the Levites, which we have in the 3d and 4th chapters of Numbers, which very much consisted in their charge of the several parts and utensils of the tabernacle. But those laws were now abolished; and they were no more to carry those things, as they had been used to do. But David appointed them to other work instead of it; 1 Chron. 23:26. "And also unto the Levites, they shall no more carry the tabernacle, nor any vessels of it for the service thereof:" a sure evidence that the ceremonial law given by Moses is not perpetual, as the Jews suppose; but might be wholly abolished by Christ: for if David, a type of the Messiah, might abolish the law of Moses in part, much more might the Messiah himself abolish the whole.

David, by God's appointment, abolished all use of the tabernacle built by Moses, and of which he had the pattern, from God: for God now revealed it to David to be his will, that a temple should be built instead of the tabernacle. This was a great presage of what Christ, the Son of David, would do when he should come, viz. abolish the whole Jewish ecclesiastical constitution, which was but as a movable tabernacle, to set up the spiritual gospel-temple, which was to be far more glorious, of greater extent, and was to last for ever. David had the pattern of all things pertaining to the temple showed him, even in like manner as Moses had the pattern of the tabernacle: and Solomon built the temple according to that pattern which he had from his father David, which he received from God. 1 Chron. 28:11-12.

> Then David gave to Solomon his son the pattern of the porch, and of the houses thereof, and of the treasuries thereof, and of the upper chambers thereof, and of the inner parlours thereof, and of the place of the mercy-seat, and the pattern of all that he had by the Spirit, of the courts of the house of the Lord, and of all the chambers round about, of the treasuries of the house of God, and of the treasuries of the dedicated things.

And, ver. 19. "All this, said David, the Lord made me understand in writing by his hand upon me, even all the works of this pattern."

**X.** The canon of Scripture seems at or after the close of David's reign to be added to by the prophets Nathan and Gad. It appears probable by the Scriptures, that they carried on the history of the two books of Samuel from the place where Samuel left it, and finished them. These seem to be called the book of Samuel the seer, and Nathan the prophet, and God the seer, 1 Chron. 29:29. "Now the acts of David the king, first and last, behold, they are written in the book of Samuel the seer, and in the book of Nathan the prophet, and in the book of Gad the seer."

**XI.** The next thing I would notice, is God's wonderful-

ly continuing the kingdom of his visible people in the
line of Christ's legal ancestors, as long as they remained
an independent kingdom. Thus it was without any interruption worth notice. Indeed the kingdom of all the
tribes of Israel was not kept in that line; but the dominion of that part in which the true worship of God
was upheld, who were God's visible people, was always
kept in the family of David, as long as there was any
such thing as an independent king of Israel; according
to his promise to David; and not only in the family
of David, but always in that part of David's posterity
whence Christ was legally descended. So that Christ's
legal ancestor was always on the throne, excepting Je-
hoahaz, who reigned three months, and Zedekiah; as
you may see in Matthew's genealogy of Christ.

Christ was legally descended from the kings of Judah,
though not naturally. He was both legally and naturally
descended from David He was naturally descended from
Nathan the son of David; for Mary his mother was one
of the posterity of David by Nathan, as you may see
in Luke's genealogy: but Joseph, the reputed and legal
father of Christ, was naturally descended of Solomon
and his successors, as we have an account in Matthew's
genealogy. Jesus Christ, though he was not the natural
son of Joseph, yet by the law and constitution of the
Jews, was Joseph's heir; because he was the lawful son of
Joseph's lawful life, conceived while she was his legally
espoused wife. The Holy Ghost raised up seed to him.
A person, by the law of Moses, might be the legal son
and heir of another, whose natural son he was not; as

sometimes a man raised up seed to his brother. a brother, in some cases, was to build up a brother's house; so the Holy Ghost built up Joseph's house. Joseph being in the direct line of the kings of Judah, of the house of David, he was in this respect the legal heir of the crown of David; and Christ being legally his first-born son, he was his heir; and so Christ, by the law, was the proper heir of the crown of David, and is therefore said to sit upon the throne of his father David.

The crown of God's people was wonderfully kept in the line of Christ's legal ancestors. When David was old, and not able any longer to manage the affairs of the kingdom, Adonijah, one of his sons, set up to be king, and seemed to have obtained his purpose. All things for a while seemed fair on his side, and he thought himself strong. But Adonijah was not the ancestor of Joseph, the legal father of Christ; and therefore how wonderfully did Providence work here! what a strange and sudden revolution! All Adonijah's kingdom and glory vanished away as soon as it was begun; and Solomon, the legal ancestor of Christ, was established in the throne.

And after Solomon's death, when Jeroboam had conspired against the family, and Rehoboam carried himself in such a manner that it was a wonder all Israel was not provoked to forsake him, (as ten tribes actually did,) and set up Jeroboam in opposition to him; and though he was a wicked man, and deserved to have been rejected altogether from being king; yet he being the legal ancestor of Christ, God kept the kingdom of the two tribes, in which the true religion was upheld, in his possession.

And though his son Abijam was another wicked prince; yet God still continued the crown in the family, and gave it to Abijam's son, Asa. And afterwards, though many of the kings of Judah were very wicked men, and horribly provoked God, as particularly Jehoram, Ahaziah, Ahaz, Manasseh, and Amon; yet God did not take away the crown from their family, but gave it to their sons, because they were the ancestors of Christ. God's remembering his covenant established with David, is given as the reason why God did thus, notwithstanding their wicked lives; 1 Kings 15:4. speaking of Abijam's wickedness, it is said, 1 Kings 15:4. "Nevertheless, for David's sake did the Lord his God give him a lamp in Jerusalem, to set up his son after him, and to establish Jerusalem:" so, speaking of Jehoram's great wickedness, it is said, 2 Chron. 21:7. "Howbeit the Lord would not destroy the house of David, because of the covenant he had made with David, and as he promised to give a light unto him, and to his sons for ever."

The crown of the ten tribes was changed from one family to another continually. First, Jeroboam took it; but the crown descended only to his son Nadab. Then Baasha, who was of another family, took it; and it remained in his posterity but one generation after his death. And then Zimri, who was his servant, and not of his posterity, took it; from whom Omri, who was of another family, took it. The crown continued in his family for three successions: and then Jehu, who was of another family, took it. The crown continued in his family for three or four successions; and then Shallum, that was of another family, took it. The crown did not descend at all to his posterity; but Menahem, who was of another family, took it; and it remained in his family but one generation after him. Then Pekah, who was of another family, took it: and after him Hoshea, that was still of another family, took it. So great a difference was there between the crown of Israel and the crown of Judah; the one was continued evermore in the same family, and with very little interruption, in one right line; the other was continually tossed about from one family to another, as if it were the sport of fortune. The reason was not, because the kings of Judah, at least many of them, were better than the kings of Israel; but the one had the blessing in them; they were the ancestors of Christ, whose right it was to sit on the throne of Israel. But with the kings of Israel it was not so; and therefore Divine Providence exercised a continual care, through all the changes that happened through so many generations, and such a long space of time, to keep the crown of Judah in one direct line, in fulfillment of the everlasting covenant he had made with David, the mercies of which covenant were sure mercies; but in the other case there was no such covenant, and so no such interposing care of Providence.

And here it must not be omitted, that there was once a very strong conspiracy of the kings of Syria and Israel, in the time of that wicked king of Judah, Ahaz, to dispossess him and his family of the throne of Judah, and to set one of another family, even the son of Tabeal, on it; as Isa. 7:6. "Let us go up against Judah, and vex it, and let us make a breach therein for us, and set a king in the midst of it, even the son of Tabeal." And they seemed very likely to accomplish their purpose. There seemed to be so great a likelihood of it, that the hearts of the people sunk within them; they gave up the cause. It is said, "The heart of Ahaz and his people was moved as the trees of the wood are moved with the wind (ver 2). And on this occasion God sent the prophet Isaiah to encourage the people, and tell them that it should not come to pass. And because it looked so much like a lost cause to Ahaz and the people, therefore God directs the prophet to give them this sign of it, viz. that Christ should be born of the legal seed of Ahaz, as Isa. 7:14. "Therefore the Lord himself shall give you a sign: behold, a virgin shall conceive, and bear a son, and shall call his name Immanuel." This was a good sign, and a great confirmation of the truth of what God promised by Isaiah, viz. that the kings of Syria and Israel should never accomplish their purpose of dispossessing the family of Ahaz of the crown of Judah, and setting up the son of Tabeal; for Christ the Immanuel was to be of them.

**XII.** The building of the temple was a great type of three things, viz. of Christ, especially his human nature; of the church; and of heaven. The tabernacle seemed rather to represent the church in its movable, changeable state, in this world. But that beautiful, glorious, costly structure, the temple, that succeeded the tabernacle, seems especially to represent the church in its glorified state in heaven. This temple was built according to the direction and the pattern shown by the Holy Ghost to David, in the place where was the threshing-floor of Oman the Jebusite, in mount Moriah, 2 Chron. 3:1.; the same mountain (and probably in the very same place) where Abraham offered up his son Isaac; for that is said to be in the land of Moriah, Gen. 22:2 and was called the mountain of the Lord, as this of the temple was, Gen. 22:14. "And Abraham called the name of that place Jehovah-jireh; as it is said to this day, In the mount of the Lord it shall be seen." This was the house where Christ dwelt, till he came to dwell in human nature. That his body was the antitype of this temple, appears from what he says, "Destroy this temple, and in three days I will raise it up," speaking of the temple of his body. This continued to be the house of God, the place of worship for his church, till Christ came; the place that God chose, where all their sacrifices were offered up, till the great sacrifice came. Into this temple the Lord came, even the messenger of the covenant. Here he often delivered his heavenly doctrine, and wrought miracles; here his church was gathered by the pouring out of the Spirit, after his ascension. Luke 24:53. "And they were continually in the temple, praising and blessing God." And respecting the multitudes that were converted by that great effusion of the Spirit on the day of Pentecost, it is said, Acts 2:46. "And they continued daily with one accord in the temple." And the sacred historian, speaking of the apostles, says, Acts 5:42. "And daily in the temple, and in every house, they ceased not to teach and preach

Jesus Christ!" And thence the sound of the gospel went forth, and the church was spread into all the world.

**XIII.** It is here worthy to be observed, that in Solomon's reign, after the temple was finished, the Jewish church was risen to its highest external glory. The Jewish church, as to its ordinances and constitution, is compared to the moon, Rev. 12:1. "And there appeared a great wonder in heaven, a woman clothed with the sun, and the moon under her feet, and upon her head a crown of twelve stars." This church was like the moon in many other respects, but especially that it waxed and waned like the moon. From its first formation, which was in the covenant made with Abraham, when this moon began to appear, it had been gradually increasing in its glory. This time, wherein the temple was finished and dedicated, was about the middle between the calling of Abraham and the coming of Christ, and now it was full moon. After this the glory of the Jewish church gradually decreased, till Christ came; as I shall have occasion to show more particularly.

Now the church of Israel was in its highest external glory. Now Israel was multiplied exceedingly, so that they seemed to have become like the sand on the sea-shore, 1 Kings 4:20. Now the kingdom of Israel was firmly established in the right family, the family of which Christ was to come. Now God had chosen the city where he would place his name; and had fully given his people the possession of the promised land.—They now possessed the dominion of it all, in quietness and peace, even from the river of Egypt, to the great river Euphrates; all those nations which had formerly been their enemies, quietly submitted to them; none pretended to rebel against them. Now the Jewish worship in all its ordinances was fully settled: instead of a movable tabernacle, they had a glorious temple; the most magnificent, beautiful, and costly structure, that ever had been, or has been since. Now the people enjoyed peace and plenty, and sat every man under his vine and fig-tree, eating and drinking and making merry, 1 Kings 4:20. They were in the highest pitch of earthly prosperity, silver being as plenty as stones, and the land full of gold and precious stones, and other precious foreign commodities, which were brought by Solomon's ships from Ophir and other parts of the world. Now they had a king reigning over them who was the wisest of men, and probably the greatest earthly prince that ever was: their fame went abroad into all the earth, so that they came from the utmost parts of the earth to see their glory and their happiness.

Thus God was pleased, in one of Messiah's ancestors, remarkably to shadow forth the kingdom of Christ and himself reigning in his glory. David, a man of war, a man who had shed much blood, and whose life was full of troubles and conflicts, was a more suitable representation of Christ in his state of humiliation, wherein he was conflicting with his enemies. But Solomon, a man of peace, was a representation more especially of Christ exalted, triumphing and reigning in his kingdom of peace. And the happy glorious state of the Jewish church at that time, remarkably represented two things:—1. A glorious state of the church on earth, in the latter ages of the world; those days of peace, when nation shall not lift sword against nation, nor learn war any more. 2. The future glorified state of the church in heaven. The earthly Canaan never was so lively a type of the heavenly Canaan as it was then, when the happy people of Israel indeed enjoyed it as a land flowing with milk and honey.

**XIV.** After this the glory of the Jewish church gradually declined more and more till Christ came; yet the work of redemption went on. Whatever failed or declined, God still carried on this work from age to age; this building was advancing higher and higher. It went on, even during the decline of the Jewish church, towards a further preparation of things for the coming of Christ, as well as during its increase; for so wonderfully were things ordered by the infinitely wise Governor of the world, that whatever happened was ordered for good to this general design, and made a means of promoting it. When the Jews flourished, and were in prosperity, he made that to contribute to the promoting of this design; and when they were in adversity, God made this also contribute to the same. While the Jewish church was in its increasing state, the work of redemption was carried on by their increase; and when they came to their declining state, from Solomon's time till Christ, God carried on the work of redemption by that. The very decline itself, was one thing that God employed as a further preparation for Christ's coming.

As the moon, from the time of its full, is approaching nearer and nearer to her conjunction with the sun; so her light is still more and more decreasing, till at length, when the conjunction comes, it is wholly swallowed up in the light of the sun. So it was with the Jewish church from the time of its highest glory in Solomon's time. In the latter end of Solomon's reign, the state of things began to darken, by his corrupting himself with idolatry, which much obscured the glory of this mighty and wise prince; and troubles also began to arise in his kingdom. After his death the kingdom was divided, and ten tribes revolted, and withdrew their subjection from the house of David, apostatizing also from the true worship of God in the temple at Jerusalem, and setting up the golden calves of Bethel and Dan. And presently after this the number of the ten tribes was greatly diminished in the battle of Jeroboam with Abijah, wherein there fell down slain of Israel five hundred thousand chosen men; which loss the kingdom of Israel probably never in any measure recovered.

The ten tribes finally apostatized from the true God under Jeroboam. The kingdom of Judah was greatly corrupted, and from that time forward more generally in a corrupt state than otherwise. In Ahab's time the kingdom of Israel did not only worship the calves of Bethel and Dan, but the worship of Baal was introduced. Before, they pretended to worship the true God by these images, the calves of Jeroboam; but now Ahab introduced gross idolatry, and the direct worship of false gods in the room of the true God; and soon after, the worship of Baal was introduced into the kingdom of Judah, viz. in Jehoram's reign, by his marrying Athaliah, the daughter of Ahab. After this God began to cut Israel short, by finally destroying and sending into captivity that part which was beyond Jordan, 2 Kings 10:32, &c. Then Tiglath-Pileser subdued and enslaved all the northern parts, 2 Kings 15:29; and at last all the ten tribes were subdued by Salmaneser, and they were finally carried away captive out of their own land. After this also the kingdom of Judah was carried captive into Babylon, and a great part of the nation never returned. Those who returned were but a small number, compared with what had been carried captive; and for the most part after this they were dependent on the power of other states. They were subject one while to the Kings of Persia, then to the monarchy of the Grecians, and then to the Romans. And before Christ's time, the Jewish church was become exceeding corrupt, overrun with superstition and self-righteousness. And how small a flock was the church of Christ in the days of his incarnation!

God, by this gradual decline of the Jewish state and church from Solomon's time, prepared the way for the coming of Christ several ways.

**1.** The decline of the glory of this legal dispensation, made way for the introduction of the more glorious dispensation of the gospel. The evangelical dispensation was so much more glorious, that the legal dispensation had no glory in comparison with it. The ancient dispensation, even as it was in Solomon's time, was but an inferior glory, compared with the spiritual glory of the dispensation introduced by Christ. The church, under the Old Testament, was a child under tutors and governors, and God dealt with it accordingly. Those pompous externals are called by the apostle, weak and beggarly elements. It was fit that those things should be diminished as Christ approached; as John the Baptist, the forerunner of Christ, speaking of Christ, says, John 3:30. "He must increase, but I must decrease." It is fit that the twinkling stars should gradually withdraw their glory, when the sun is approaching towards his rising point. The glory of the Jewish dispensation must be gradually diminished, to prepare the way for the more joyful reception of the spiritual glory of the gospel. If the Jewish church, when Christ came, had been in the same external glory that it was in, in the reign of Solomon, men would have their eyes so dazzled with it, that they would not have been likely, joyfully to exchange such great external grandeur, for only the spiritual glory of the despised Jesus. Again,

**2.** This gradual decline of the glory in the Jewish state, tended to make the glory of God's power, in the great effects of Christ's redemption, the more conspicuous. God's people being so diminished and weakened by one step after another, till Christ came, was very much like the diminishing of Gideon's army. God told Gideon, that the people with him were too many for the conquest of the Midianites, lest Israel should vaunt itself, saying, "My own hand hath saved me. "And therefore all that were fearful were commanded to return; and there returned twenty and two thousand, and there remained ten thousand. But still they were too many; and then, by trying the people at the water, they were reduced to three hundred men. So the people in Solomon's time were too many, and mighty, and glorious for Christ; therefore he diminished them; first, by sending off the ten tribes; then he diminished them by the captivity into Babylon; and then they were further diminished by their great and general corruption when Christ came; so that Christ found very few godly persons among them. With a small handful of disciples, Christ conquered the world. Thus high things were brought down, that Christ might be exalted.

**3.** This prepared the way for Christ's coming, as it made the salvation of those Jews who were saved by Christ to he more sensible and visible. Though the greater part of the Jewish nation was rejected, and the Gentiles called in their room; yet a great many thousands of the Jews were saved by Christ after his resurrection, Acts 21:20. They being taken from so low a state under temporal calamity in their bondage to the Romans, and from a state of so great superstition and wickedness, it made their redemption the more sensibly and visibly glorious.

**XV.** I would here take notice of the additions which were made to the canon of Scripture in or soon after the reign of Solomon. There were considerable additions made by Solomon himself, who wrote the books of Proverbs and Ecclesiastes, probably near the close of his reign. His Song of Songs, as it is called, is wholly on the subject we are upon, viz. Christ and his redemption, representing the high and glorious relation, union, and love, that is between Christ and his redeemed church. And the sacred history seems, in Solomon's reign, and some of the next succeeding, to have been enlarged by the prophets Nathan and Ahijah, Shemaiah and Iddo. It is probable that part of the history which we have in the first of Kings, was written by them. (See 2 Chron. 9:29, 12:15, 13:22).

**XVI.** God wonderfully upheld his church and the true religion through this period. It was very wonderful, considering the many and great apostasies of that people to idolatry. When the ten tribes had generally and finally forsaken the true worship, God kept up the true religion in the kingdom of Judah; and when they corrupted themselves, as they very often did exceedingly, and idolatry was ready totally to swallow up all, yet God kept the lamp alive. When things seemed to be come to an extremity, and religion at its last gasp, he was often pleased to grant blessed revivals by remarkable outpourings of his Spirit, particularly in Hezekiah's and Josiah's time.

**XVII.** God remarkably kept the book of the law from being lost in times of general and long-continued neglect of it. The most remarkable instance of this kind was its preservation in the time of the great apostasy, during the greatest part of the long reign of Manasseh, which lasted fifty-five years, and the reign of Amon his son. This while the law was so much neglected, and such a careless and profane management of the affairs of the temple prevailed, that the book which used to be laid up by the side of the ark in the Holy of Holies, was lost for a long time; and nobody knew where it was. But yet God preserved it from being finally lost. In Josiah's time, when they came to repair the temple, it was found buried in rubbish. It had been lost so long that Josiah himself seems to have been much a stranger to it. (See 2 Kings 22:8., &c.)

**XVIII.** God remarkably preserved the tribe of which Christ was to proceed, from being mined through the many and great dangers of this period. The visible church of Christ from Solomon's reign was mainly in the tribe of Judah. The tribe of Benjamin, which was annexed to them, was but a very small tribe, and that of Judah exceeding large; and as Judah took Benjamin under his protection when he went into Egypt to bring corn, so the tribe of Benjamin seemed to be under the covert of Judah ever after. And though, on occasion of Jeroboam's setting up the calves at Bethel and Dan, the Levites resorted to Judah out of all the tribes of Israel, (2 Chron. 11:13.) yet they were also small, and not reckoned among the tribes. Many of the ten tribes, it is true, on that occasion, for the sake of worshipping God in the temple, left their inheritances in their several tribes, and settled in Judah, and so were incorporated with them, as we have account in the chapter just quoted, (2 Chron. 11:16.) yet the tribe of Judah was so much the prevailing part, that they were called by one name, Judah. Therefore God said to Solomon, 1 Kings 11:13. "I will not rend away all the kingdom: but will give one tribe to thy son, for David my servant's sake, and for Jerusalem's sake, which I have chosen." So when the ten tribes were carried captive, it is said, there was none left but the tribe of Judah: 2 Kings 17:18. "Therefore the Lord was very wroth with Israel, and removed them out of his sight: there was none left but the tribe of Judah only." Whence they were all called Jews, a word derived from Judah.

This was the tribe of which Christ was to come; and in this chiefly did God's visible church consist, from Solomon's time. This people, over whom the kings who were legal ancestors of Christ, and of the house of David, reigned, was wonderfully preserved from destruction during this period, when they often seemed to be upon the brink of ruin, and just ready to be swallowed up. So it was in Rehoboam's time, when Shishak king of Egypt came against Judah with a vast force. Of this we read in the beginning of 2 Chronicles 12. So it was again in Abijah's time, when Jeroboam set the battle in array against him with eight hundred thousand chosen men; a mighty army! 2 Chron. 13:3. Then God wrought deliverance to Judah, out of regard to the covenant of grace established with David, as is evident by 2 Chron. 13:4-5. and the victory they obtained was because the Lord was on their side, as you may see, 2 Chron. 13:2. So it was again in Asa's time, when Zerah the Ethiopian came against him with a larger army of a thousand and three hundred chariots, 2 Chron. 14: 9. On this occasion Asa cried to the Lord, and trusted in him, being sensible that it was nothing with him to help those that had no power: 2 Chron. 14: 11. "And Asa cried unto the Lord his God, and said, Lord, it is nothing with thee to help, whether with many, or with those that have no power." And accordingly God gave them a glorious victory over this mighty host.

So again it was in Jehoshaphat's time, when the children of Moab, and the children of Ammon, and the inhabitants of mount Seir, combined together against Judah with a mighty army, a force vastly superior to any that Jehoshaphat could raise; and Jehoshaphat and his people were greatly afraid: yet they set themselves to seek God on this occasion, and trusted in him; and God told them by one of his prophets, that they need not fear them, nor should they have any occasion to fight in this battle, they should only stand still and see the salvation of the Lord. And according to his direction, they only stood still, and sang praises to God; and God made their enemies do the work themselves, by killing one another; and the children of Judah had nothing to do, but to gather the spoil, which was more than they could carry away. (2 Chron. 20.)

So it was again in Ahaz's time, when Rezin the king of Syria, and Pekah the son of Remaliah, the king of Israel, conspired against Judah, and seemed to be sure of their purpose; of which we have spoken already. So it was again in Hezekiah's time, when Sennacherib, that great king of Assyria, and head of the greatest monarchy then in the world, came up against all the fenced cities of Judah, after he had conquered most of the neighbouring countries. He sent Rabshakeh, the captain of his host, against Jerusalem, who in a very proud and scornful manner insulted Hezekiah and his people, as being sure of victory; and the people were trembling for fear, like lambs before a lion. Then God sent Isaiah the prophet to comfort them, and assure them that their enemies should not prevail; as a token of which he gave them this sign, viz. that the earth, for two years successively, should bring forth food of itself, from the roots of the old stalks, without their ploughing or sowing; and then the third year they should sow and reap, and plant vineyards, and eat the fruit of them, and live on the fruits of their labour, as they were wont to do before. (See 2 Kings 19:29.) This is mentioned as a type of what is promised in 2 Kings 19:30-31. "And the remnant that is escaped of the house of Judah, shall yet again take root downward, and bear fruit upward. For out of Jerusalem shall go forth a remnant, and they that escape, out of mount Zion: the zeal of the Lord of hosts shall do this." The corn springing again after it had been cut off with the sickle, and bringing forth another crop from the roots, represents the church reviving again, and flourishing, like a plant after it had seemingly been cut down past recovery. When the enemies of the church have done their utmost, and seem to have gained their point; when they have overthrown the church, so that its being is scarcely visible, but is like a living root hid under ground; there is in it a secret life that will cause it to flourish again, and to take root downward, and bear fruit upward. This was now fulfilled. The king of Assyria had already carried captive the ten tribes; and

Sennacherib had also taken all the fenced cities of Judah, and ranged the country round about, and Jerusalem only remained: and Rabshakeh had in his own imagination already swallowed that up, as he had also in the fearful apprehensions of the Jews themselves. But God wrought a wonderful deliverance; he sent an angel, that in one night smote a hundred fourscore and five thousand in the enemy's camp.

**XIX.** In the reign of Uzziah, and the following reigns, God was pleased to raise up a set of eminent prophets, who should commit their prophecies to writing, and leave them for the use of his church in all ages. We before observed, how that God began a constant succession of prophets in Israel in Samuel's time, and many of these prophets wrote by divine inspiration, and so added to the canon of Scripture. But none of them are supposed to have written books of prophecies till now. Several of them wrote histories of the wonderful dispensations of God towards his church. This we have observed already of Samuel, who is supposed to have written Judges and Ruth, and part of the first of Samuel, if not the book of Joshua. And Nathan and Gad seem to have written the rest of the two books of Samuel: and Nathan, with Ahijah and Iddo, wrote the history of Solomon, which is probably that which we have in the first book of Kings. The history of Israel seems to have been further carried on by Iddo and Shemaiah: 2 Chron. 12: 15. "Now the acts of Rehoboam, first and last, are they not written in the book of Shemaiah the prophet, and Iddo the seer, concerning genealogies ?" And after that the history seems to been further carried on by the prophet Jehu, the son of Hanani: 2 Chron. 20:34. " Now the rest of the acts of Jehoshaphat, first and last, behold they are written in the book of Jehu son of Hanani, who is mentioned in the book of the kings of Israel." 1 Kings 16: 1, 7. And then it was further continued by the prophet Isaiah: 2 Chron. 26:22. "Now the rest of the acts of Uzziah, first and last, did Isaiah the prophet the son of Amos write." He probably did it as well in the second book of Kings, as in the book of his prophecy. And the history was carried on and finished by other prophets after him.

Thus the prophets, even from Samuel's time, had been adding to the canon of Scripture by their historical writings. But now, in the days of Uzziah, did God first raise up a set of great prophets, not only to write histories, but to write books of their prophecies. The first of these is thought to be Hosea the son of Beeri, and therefore his prophecy, or the word of the Lord by him, is called the beginning of the word the Lord; Hos. 1:2, "The beginning of the word of the Lord by Hosea;" that is, the beginning, or the first part, of the written word of that kind, viz. that which is written in books of prophecy. He prophesied in the days of Uzziah, Jotham, Ahaz, and Hezekiah, kings of Judah, and in the days of Jeroboam, the son of Joash, king of Israel. There were many other witnesses for God raised up about the same time to commit their prophecies to writing, Isaiah, Amos, Jonah, Micah, Nahum, and probably some others: and so from that time forward God seemed to continue a succession of writing prophets.

This was a great dispensation of Providence, and a great advance made in the affair of redemption, which will appear, if we consider, that the main business of the prophets was to point out Christ and his redemption. They were all forerunners of the great prophet. The main end why the spirit of prophecy was given them was, that they might give testimony to Jesus Christ, the great Redeemer, who was to come. Therefore, the testimony of Jesus, and the spirit of prophecy, are spoken of as the same thing; Rev. 19:10. "And I fell at his feet to worship him: and he said unto me, See thou do it not: I am thy fellow servant, and of thy brethren that have the testimony of Jesus: worship God: for the testimony of Jesus is the spirit of prophecy."

And therefore we find, that the great and main thing that the most of the prophets in their written prophecies insist upon, is Christ and his redemption, and the glorious times of the gospel. And though many other things were spoken of in their prophecies, yet they seem to be only as introductory to their prophecy of these great things. Whatever they predict, here their prophecies commonly terminate.

These prophets, inspired by the Spirit of Christ, wrote chiefly to prepare the way for his coming, and to exhibit the glory that should follow. And in what an exalted strain do they all speak of those things! Many other things they speak of in men's usual language. But when they enter upon this subject, what a joyful heavenly sublimity is there in their language! Some of them are very particular and full in their predictions of these things, and above all the prophet Isaiah, who is therefore deservedly called the evangelical prophet. He seems to teach the glorious doctrines of the gospel almost as plainly as the apostles did. The apostle Paul therefore takes notice, that the prophet Esaias is very bold, Rom. 10:20. i.e. according to the meaning of the word in the New Testament, is very plain, he speaks out very plainly and fully; so being very bold is used 2 Cor. 3:12. we use great boldness of speech, or boldness, as in the margin.

How plainly and fully does the prophet Isaiah describe the manner and circumstances, the nature and end, of the sufferings and sacrifice of Christ, in the 53rd chapter of his prophecy. There is scarce a chapter in the New Testament itself which is more full upon it. And how much, and in what a glorious strain, does the same prophet speak, from time to time, of the glorious benefits of Christ, the unspeakable blessings which shall redound to his church through his redemption! Jesus Christ, of whom this prophet spoke so much, once appeared to him in the form of the human nature, the nature he should afterwards take upon him. We have an account of it in Isaiah 6 at the beginning: Isaiah 6:1. "I saw also the Lord sitting on a throne, high and lifted up, and his train filled the temple," &c. This was Christ, as we are expressly told in the New Testament. (See John 12:39-41. )

And if we consider the abundant prophecies of this and the other prophets, what a great increase is there of gospel light! How plentiful are the revelations and prophecies of Christ, compared with what they were in the first period of the Old Testament, from Adam to Noah; or to what they were in the second, from Noah to Abraham; or to what they were before Moses, or in the time of Moses, Joshua, and the Judges! This dispensation was also a glorious advance of the work of redemption by the great additions that were made to the canon of scripture. A great part of the Old Testament was written now from the days of Uzziah to the captivity into Babylon. And how excellent are those portions of it! What a precious treasure have those prophets committed to the church of God, tending greatly to confirm the gospel of Christ! and which has been of great comfort and benefit to God's church in all ages since, and doubtless will be to the end of the world.

## 1.6 PART VI

### 7.0 from the Babylonish captivity to the coming of Christ.

I COME NOW to the last subordinate period of the Old Testament, viz. that which begins with the Babylonish captivity, and extends to the coming of Christ, being near six hundred years; and shall endeavour to show how the work of redemption was carried on through this period.—But before I enter upon particulars, I would observe three things wherein this period is distinguished from the preceding ones.

**1.** Though we have no account of a great part of this period in the scripture history, yet the events of it are more the subject of scripture prophecy, than any of the preceding periods. There are two ways wherein the Scriptures give account of the events by which the work of redemption is carried on; one is by history, and another is by prophecy; and in one or the other of these ways we have in the Scriptures an account how the work of redemption is carried on from the beginning to the end. Although the Scriptures do not contain a proper history of the whole, yet the whole chain of great events, by which this affair hath been carried on from the commencement to the finishing of it, is found either in history or prophecy. And it is to be observed, that where the Scripture is wanting in one of these ways, it is made up in the other. Where scripture history fails, there prophecy takes place; so that the account is still carried on, and the chain is not broken, till we come to the very last link of it in the consummation of all things.

And accordingly it is observable of this space of time, that though it is so much less the subject of scripture history, than most of the preceding periods, (there being above four hundred years of which the Scriptures give us no history,) yet its events are more the subject of prophecy, than those of all the preceding periods put together. Most of those remarkable prophecies of the book of Daniel, and most of those in Isaiah, Jeremiah, and Ezekiel, against Babylon, Tyrus, Egypt, and many other nations, were fulfilled in this period.

Hence the reason why the Scriptures give us no history of so great a part of this time, is not because the events were not so important, or less worthy of notice, than those of the foregoing periods; for they were great and remarkable. But there are several reasons which may be given for it. One is, that it was the will of God that the spirit of prophecy should cease in this period, (for reasons that may be given hereafter,) so that there were no prophets to write the history of these times; and therefore God designing this, took care that the great events of this period should not be without mention in his word. It is observable, that the writing prophets in Israel, were raised up at the latter end of the foregoing period, and at the beginning of this; for the time was now approaching, when, the spirit of prophecy having ceased, there was to be no inspired history, and therefore no other scripture account but what was given in prophecy.

Another reason may be, for the suspension of inspired history, that God in his providence took care, that there should be authentic and full accounts of the events of this period preserved in profane history. It is very worthy of notice, that with respect to the events of the five preceding subordinate periods, of which the Scriptures give the history, profane history gives us no account, or at least of but very few of them. There are many fabulous and uncertain accounts of things that happened before; but the commencement of authentic profane history is judged to be but about a hundred years before Nebuchadnezzar's time. The learned Greeks and Romans used to call the ages before that the fabulous age; but the times after that they called the historical age. And from about that time to the coming of Christ, we have undoubted accounts in profane history of the principal events; accounts that wonderfully agree with the many prophecies that relate to those times.

Thus the great God, who disposes all things, took care to give an historical account of things from the beginning of the world, through all those former ages concerning which profane history is silent; and ceased not till he came to those ages in which profane history related things with some certainty. And concerning those times he gives us abundant account in prophecy, that by comparing profane history with those prophecies, we might see the agreement.

**2.** This last period of the Old Testament seems to have been remarkably distinguished from all others by great revolutions among the nations of the earth, to make way for the kingdom of Christ. The time now drawing nigh wherein Christ, the great King and Saviour of the world, was to come, great and mighty were the changes that were brought to pass in order to it. The way had been preparing for the coming of Christ from the fall of man, through all the foregoing periods; but now, the time drawing nigh, things began to ripen apace for his coming; and therefore Divine Providence now wrought wonderfully. The greatest revolutions that any history has recorded, since the flood, fell out in this period. Almost all the nations far and near, within the knowledge of the Jews, were overturned again and again. All lands were in their turn subdued, captivated, and as it were emptied, and turned upside down, and that most of them repeatedly, in this period; agreeable to that prophecy, Isa. 24:1. "Behold, the Lord maketh the earth empty; he maketh it waste, and turneth it upside down, and scattereth abroad the inhabitants thereof."

This began with God's visible church, in their captivity by the king of Babylon. And then the cup from them went round to all other nations, agreeable to what God revealed to the prophet Jeremiah 25:15-27. Here special respect seems to be had to the great revolutions in the times of the Babylonish empire. But after that there were three general overturnings before Christ came, in the succession of the three great monarchies of the world, after the Babylonish empire. The king of Babylon is represented in Scripture as overturning the world: but after that, the Babylonish empire was overthrown by Cyrus, who founded the Persian empire in the room of it; which was of much greater extent than the Babylonish empire in its greatest glory. Thus the world was overturned the second time. And then, the Persian empire was overthrown by Alexander, and the Grecian set up, which was still of much greater extent than the Persian. And thus there was a general overturning of the world a third time. After that, the Grecian empire was overthrown by the Romans, and the Roman empire was established; which vastly exceeded all the foregoing empires in power and extent of dominion. And so the world was overturned the fourth time.

These several monarchies, and the great revolutions of the world under them, are abundantly spoken of in the prophecies of Daniel. They are represented in Nebuchadnezzar's image of gold, silver, brass, and iron, and Daniel's interpretation of it, (Dan. 2 ) in the vision of the four beasts, and the angel's interpretation of it, (Dan. 7 ) And the succession of the Persian and Grecian monarchies is more particularly represented in the 8th chapter, in Daniel's vision of the ram and the he-goat, and again in the 11th chapter.

Beside these four general overturnings, the world was kept in a constant tumult between whiles; and indeed in a continual convulsion through this whole period. Before, the face of the earth was comparatively in quietness; though there were many great wars among the nations, yet we read of no such mighty and universal convulsions and overturnings as there were in this period. The nations of the world, most of them, had long remained on their lees, without being emptied from vessel to vessel, as is said of Moab, Jer. 18:11. Now these great overturnings were because the time of the great Messiah drew nigh. That they were to prepare the way for Christ's coming, is evident by Scripture, particularly by Ezek. 21:27. "I will overturn, overturn, overturn it, and it shall be no more, until he come whose right it is, and I will give it him." The prophet, by repealing the word overturn three times, has respect to three overturnings, as in the Revelation 8:13. The repetition of the word woe three times, signifies three distinct woes; as appears by what follows, Revelation 9:12. "One woe is past;" and Revelation 11:14. "The second woe is past, and behold the third woe cometh quickly."

It must be noted, that the prophet Ezekiel prophesied in the time of the Babylonish captivity; and therefore there were three great and general overturnings to come after this prophecy, before Christ came; the first by the Persians, the second by the Grecians, the third by the Romans; and then Christ, whose right it was to take the diadem, and reign, should come. Here these great overturnings are evidently spoken of as preparatory to the coming and kingdom of Christ. But to understand the words aright, we must note the particular expression, "I will overturn, overturn, overturn it," i.e. the diadem and crown of Israel, or the supreme temporal dominion over God's visible people. This God said should be no more, i.e. the crown should be taken off, and the diadem removed, as it is said in the foregoing verse. The supreme power over Israel should be no more in the royal line of David, to which it properly belonged, but should be removed away, and given to others, and overturned from one to another: first the supreme power over Israel should be in the hands of the Persians; then it should be overturned, and be in the hands of the Grecians; and then it should be overturned again, and come into the hands of the Romans, and be no more in the line of David, till that very person should come, who was the Son of David, whose proper right it was, and then God would give it to him.

That those great shakings and revolutions of the nations of the world, were all to prepare the way for Christ's coming, and setting up his kingdom in the world, is further manifest by Haggai 2:6- 7. "For thus saith the Lord of hosts, Yet once, it is a little while, and I will shake the heavens, and the earth, and the sea and the dry land: and I will shake all nations, and the desire of all nations shall come, and I will fill this house with glory, saith the Lord of hosts." And again, Haggai 2: 21-23. It is evident by this, that these great revolutions and shakings of the nations, whereby the thrones of kingdoms and their armies were overthrown, and every one came down by the sword of his brother, were to prepare the way for the coming of him who is the desire of all nations.

The great changes and troubles that have sometimes been in the visible church of Christ, (Rev. 12:2. ) are compared to the church's being in travail to bring forth Christ: so these great troubles and mighty revolutions, were, as it were, the world's being in travail to bring forth the Son of God. The apostle, in the 8th of Romans, represents the whole creation as groaning and travailing in pain together until now, to bring forth the liberty and manifestation of the children of God.—So the world as it were travailed in pain, and was in continual convulsions, for several hundred years together, to bring forth the first-born child, and the only-begotten Son of God. And those mighty revolutions were as so many pangs and throes in order to it. The world being so long a time kept in a state of war and bloodshed, prepared the way for the coming of the Prince of peace, as it showed the great need the world stood in of such a prince, to deliver the world from its miseries.

It pleased God to order it in his providence, that earthly power and dominion should be raised to its greatest height, and appear in its utmost glory, in those four great monarchies that succeeded one another, and that every one should be greater and more glorious than the preceding, before he set up the kingdom of his Son. By this it appeared how much more glorious his spiritual kingdom was than the most glorious temporal kingdom. The strength and glory of Satan's kingdom in these four mighty monarchies, appeared in its greatest height: for, being the monarchies of the heathen world, the strength of them was the strength of Satan's kingdom. God suffered Satan's kingdom to rise to so great a height of power and magnificence before his Son came to overthrow it, in order to prepare the way for the more glorious triumph of his Son. Goliath must have on all his splendid armour when the stripling David comes against him with a sling and a stone, for the greater glory of David's victory. God suffered one of those great monarchies to subdue another, and erect itself on the other's ruins, appearing still in greater strength, and the last to be strongest and mightiest of all; that so Christ, in overthrowing that, might as it were overthrow them all at once. The stone cut out of the mountain without hands, is represented as destroying the whole image, the gold, the silver, the brass, the iron, and the clay; so that all became as the chaff of the summer threshing-floor.

These mighty empires were suffered thus to overthrow the world, and destroy one another. And though their power was so great, yet they could not uphold themselves, but fell one after another, and came to nothing; even the last of them, which was the strongest, and had swallowed up the earth. It pleased God thus to show in them the instability and vanity of all earthly power and greatness; which served as a foil to set forth the glory of the kingdom of his Son, which never shall be destroyed, Dan 2:44. "In the days of these kings shall the God of heaven set up a kingdom, which shall never be destroyed; and the kingdom shall not be left to other people, but it shall break in pieces and consume all these kingdoms, and it shall stand for ever." So greatly does this kingdom differ from all those kingdoms: they vanish away, and are left to other people; but this shall not be so left, but shall stand for ever. God suffered the devil to do his utmost, and to establish his interest, by setting up the greatest, strongest, and most glorious kingdoms in the world, before the despised Jesus overthrew him and his empire. Christ came into the world to bring down the high things of Satan's kingdom, that the hand of the Lord might be on every one that is proud and lofty, and every high tower, and every lofty mountain; as the prophet Isaiah says, chap, 2:12 &c. And therefore these things were suffered to rise very high, that Christ might appear so much the more glorious in being above them. Thus wonderfully did the great and wise Governor of the world prepare the way for the erecting of the glorious kingdom of his beloved Son Jesus.

**3.** Another thing for which this last space of time before Christ was particularly remarkable, was the wonderful preservation of the church through all those over-turnings. The preservation of the church was on some accounts more remarkable through this period, than through any of the foregoing. It was very wonderful that the church, which now was so weak, and in so low a state, and mostly subject to the dominion of heathen monarchies, should be preserved for five or six hundred years together, while the world was so often over-turned, and the earth was rent in pieces, and made so often empty and waste, and the inhabitants of it came down so often every one by the sword of his brother. I say, it was wonderful that the church in its weak and low state, being but a little handful of men, should be preserved in all these great convulsions; especially considering that the land of Judea, the chief place of the church's residence, lay in the midst of the contending parties, was very much the seat of war amongst them, and was often overrun and subdued. It was sometimes in the hands of one people, and sometimes another, and very much the object of the envy and hatred of all heathen nations. It was often almost ruined by them, often great multitudes of its inhabitants being slain, and the land in a great measure depopulated; and those who had them in their power, often intended the utter destruction of the whole nation. Yet they were upheld; they were preserved in their captivity in Babylon, in all the dangers they passed through under the kings of Persia, in the much greater dangers under the empire of the Greeks, and afterwards when the world was trodden down by the Romans.

Their preservation through this period was also peculiarly remarkable, in that we never read of the church suffering persecution in any former period in any measure to such a degree as they did in this, under Antiochus Epiphanes, of which more afterwards. This wonderful preservation of the church through all these overturnings of the world, gives light and confirmation to what we read in the beginning of the 46th psalm:

> God is our refuge and strength, a very present help in trouble.—Therefore will not we fear, though the earth be removed, and though the mountains be carried into the midst of the sea; though the waters thereof roar, and be troubled; though the mountains shake with the swelling thereof.

Thus I have taken notice of some general things wherein this last period of the Old-Testament times was distinguished. I come now to consider how the work of redemption was carried on in particulars.

**I.** The first thing that here offers, is the captivity of the Jews into Babylon. This was a great dispensation of Providence, and such as never was before. The children of Israel in the time of the judges, had often been brought under their enemies; and many particular persons were carried captive at other times. But never had there been any such thing as destroying the whole land, the sanctuary, and the city of Jerusalem, and all the cities and villages of the land, and carrying the whole body of the people out of their own land into a country many hundred miles distant, and leaving the land of Canaan empty of God's visible people. The ark had once forsaken the tabernacle of Shiloh, and was carried captive into the land of the Philistines: but never had there been any such thing as burning the sanctuary, utterly destroying the ark, carrying away all the sacred vessels and utensils, breaking up all their stated worship in the land, and the land lying waste and empty for so many years together. How lively are those things set forth in the Lamentations of Jeremiah! The work of redemption was promoted by this remarkable dispensation in these following ways.

**1.** It finally cured that nation of their idolatry. The prophet Isaiah, speaking of the setting up of the kingdom of Christ, speaks of the abolishing of idolatry as one thing that should be done to this end: Isaiah 2:18. "and the idols he shall utterly abolish." When the time was drawing near, that God would abolish heathen idolatry, through the greater part of the known world, as he did by the preaching of the gospel, it pleased him first to abolish heathenism among his own people; which he did by their captivity into Babylon. This was a presage of that abolition of idols, which God was about to bring to pass by Christ through so great a part of the heathen world.

This nation, that was addicted to idolatry for so many ages, notwithstanding all reproofs, warnings, corrections, and all the judgments God inflicted on them for it; were now finally cured. So that however some might fall into this sin afterwards, as they did about the time of Antiochus's persecution, yet the nation, as a nation, never showed any propensity to this sin any more. This was a remarkable and wonderful change in that people, and what directly promoted the work of redemption, as it was a great advancement of the interest of religion.

**2.** One thing that prepared the way for Christ's coming, and for setting up the glorious dispensation of the gospel, was the taking away many of those things wherein consisted the glory of the Jewish dispensation. In order to introduce the glorious dispensation of the gospel, the external glory of the Jewish church must be diminished. This the Babylonish captivity did many ways.

First, it removed the temporal dominion of the house of David, i.e. the supreme and independent government of themselves. It took away the crown and diadem from the nation. The time now approaching when Christ, the great and everlasting King of his church, was to reign, it was time for the typical kings to withdraw. As God said by Ezekiel chap. 21:26. "He removed the crown and diadem, that it might be no more, till he should come whose right it was." The Jews henceforward were always dependent on the governing power of other nations, until Christ came, for near six hundred years; except about ninety years, during which space they maintained a sort of independence by continual wars under the dominion of the Maccabees and their posterity.

Again, by the captivity, the glory and magnificence of the temple were taken away, and the temple that was built afterwards was nothing in comparison with it. Thus it was meet, that when the time drew nigh that the glorious antetype of the temple should appear, that the typical temple should have its glory withdrawn.

Moreover, they lost by the captivity the two tables of the testimony delivered to Moses, on which God with his own finger wrote the ten commandments on mount Sinai. These seem to have been preserved in the ark till the captivity.—These were in the ark when Solomon placed the ark in the temple, 1 Kings 8:9. "There was nothing in the ark, save the two tables of stone, which Moses put there at Horeb." We have no reason to suppose any other, but that they remained there as long as that temple stood. But the Jews speak of these as finally lost at that time; though the same commandments were preserved in the book of the law. These tables also were withdrawn on the approach of their antetype.

Another thing that was lost was the Urim and Thummim. This is evident by Ezra 2:63. "And the Tirshatha said unto them, that they should not eat of the most holy things, till there should stand up a priest with Urim and Thummim." We have no account that this was ever restored; though the ancient writings of the Jews say the contrary. What this Urim and Thummim was, I shall not now inquire; but only observe, that it was something by which the high priest inquired of God, and received immediate answers from him, or by which God gave forth immediate oracles on particular occasions. This was now withdrawn, the time approaching when Christ, the antetype of the Urim and Thummim, the great word and oracle of God, was to come.

Another thing that the ancient Jews say was wanting in the second temple, was the Shechinah, or cloud of glory over the mercy-seat. This was promised to be in the tabernacle: Lev. 16:2. "For I will appear in the cloud upon the mercy-seat." And we read elsewhere of the cloud of glory descending into the tabernacle, Exod. 40:35. and so we do likewise with respect to Solomon's temple. But we have no account that this cloud of glory was in the second temple. And the ancient accounts of the Jews say, that there was no such thing in the second temple. This was needless in the second temple, considering that God had promised that he would fill this temple with glory another way, viz. by Christ's coming into it; which was afterwards fulfilled. See Haggai. 2:7. "I will shake all nations and the desire of all nations shall come, and I will fill this house with glory, saith the Lord of hosts."

When Moses built the tabernacle and altar in the wilderness, and the first sacrifices were offered on it, fire came down from heaven, and consumed the burnt-offering, as in Lev. 9: 24. also when Solomon built the temple, and offered the first sacrifices, 2 Chron. 7:1. And this fire was never to go out, but to be kept alive with the greatest care, as God commanded, Lev. 6:13. "The fire shall ever be burning upon the altar; it shall never go out." And there is no reason to suppose the fire kindled in Solomon's time ever went out till the temple was destroyed by the Babylonians. But then it was extinguished, and never was restored. We have no account of its being given on building the second temple, as we have at the building of the tabernacle and first temple. But the Jews, after their return, were forced to make use of their common fire instead of it, according to the ancient tradition of the Jews. Thus the lights of the Old Testament go out on the approach of the glorious Sun of righteousness.

**3.** The captivity into Babylon occasioned the dispersion of the Jews through the greater part of the known world, before the coming of Christ. For the whole nation being carried away far out of their own land, and continuing in a state of captivity for so long a time, they got possessions, built houses, and settled themselves in the land of their captivity, agreeable to the direction that Jeremiah gave them, (Jer. 29 ) And therefore, when Cyrus gave them liberty to return to the land where they had formerly dwelt, many of them never returned; they were not willing to leave their settlements and possessions there, to go into a desolate country, many hundred miles distant, which none but the old men among them had ever seen; and therefore they were but a small number that returned, as we see in the books of Ezra and Nehemiah. Great numbers tarried behind, though they still retained the same religion with those that returned, so far as it could be practised in a foreign land. Those messengers that we read of in the 7th chapter of Zechariah, that came to inquire of the priests and prophets in Jerusalem, Sherezer and Regem-melech, are supposed to be messengers sent from the Jews that remained still in Babylon.

Those Jews who remained in that country were soon, by the great changes that happened in the world, dispersed thence into all the adjacent countries. Hence we find, that in Esther's time, which was after the return from the captivity, the Jews were dispersed throughout all parts of the vast Persian empire, which extended from India to Ethiopia; Esth. 3:8. "And Haman said unto king Ahasuerus, There is a certain people scattered abroad, and dispersed among the people in all the provinces of thy kingdom," &c. And so they continued dispersed till Christ came, and till the apostles went forth to preach the gospel. But yet these dispersed Jews retained their religion. Their captivity, as before observed, thoroughly cured them of their idolatry; and it was their manner, as many of them as could, to go up to Jerusalem at their great feasts. Hence we read in the 7th chapter of Acts, that at the great feast of Pentecost, there were Jews abiding at Jerusalem out of every nation under heaven. These had come up from all countries where they were dispersed, to worship at that feast. And hence we find, in their history, that wherever the apostles went preaching through the world, they found Jews. They came to one city, and to another city, and went into the synagogue of the Jews.

Antiochus the Great, about two hundred years before Christ, on a certain occasion, transplanted two thousand families of Jews from the country about Babylon into Asia the Less; and so they and their posterity, many of them, settled in Pontus, Galatia, Phrygia, Pamphylia, and in Ephesus; and from thence settled in Athens, and Corinth, and Rome. Whence came the synagogues in those places in which the apostle Paul preached.—Now, this dispersion of the Jews through the world before Christ came, did many ways prepare the way for his coming, and setting up his kingdom in the world.

This was a means of raising a general expectation of the Messiah through the world, about the time that he actually came. For the Jews, wherever they were dispersed, carried the Holy Scriptures with them, and so the prophecies of the Messiah; and being conversant with the nations among whom they lived, they, by that means, became acquainted with these prophecies, and with the expectations of the Jews concerning their glorious Messiah. Hence, the birth of such a glorious person in Judea, about that time, began to be the general expectation of all nations, as appears by the writings of learned heathens, which are still extant; particularly the famous poet Virgil, who lived in Italy a little before Christ, has a poem about the expectation of a great prince that was to be born, and the happy times of righteousness and peace he was to introduce; some of it very much in the language of the prophet Isaiah.

Another way by which this dispersed state of the Jews prepared the way for Christ was, that it showed the necessity of abolishing the Jewish dispensation, and introducing a new dispensation of the covenant of grace. It showed the necessity of abolishing the ceremonial law, and the old Jewish worship: for, by this means, the observance of that ceremonial law became impracticable even by the Jews themselves. The ceremonial law was adapted to the state of a people dwelling together in the same land, where was the city which God had chosen; where was the temple, the only place where they might offer sacrifices; and where alone it was lawful for their priests and Levites to officiate, where they were to bring their first-fruits, where were their cities of refuge, and the like. But by this dispersion, many of the Jews lived more than a thousand miles distant, when Christ came; which made the observance of their laws of sacrifices, and the like, impracticable. And though their forefathers might be to blame in not going up to the land of Judea when they were permitted by Cyrus, yet the case was now, as to many of them at least, become impracticable; which showed the necessity of introducing a new dispensation, that should be fitted, not only to one particular land, but to the general circumstances and use of all nations of the world.

Again, this universal dispersion of the Jews contributed to make the facts concerning Jesus Christ publicly known through the world. For, as observed before, the Jews who lived in other countries, used frequently to go up to Jerusalem at their three great feasts, from year to year; by which means, they could not but become acquainted with the wonderful things that Christ did in that land. We find that the great miracle of raising Lazarus excited the curiosity of those foreign Jews who came up at the feast of the passover to see Jesus; John 12:19-21. These Greeks were foreign Jews and proselytes, as is evident by their coming to worship at the feast of the passover. The Jews who lived abroad among the Greeks, and spoke their language, were called Greeks, Hellenists, and Grecians, Acts 6:1. These were not Gentile Christians; for this occurred before the calling of the Gentiles.

By the same means the Jews who went up from other countries became acquainted with Christ's crucifixion. Thus the disciples going to Emmaus say to Christ, whom they did not know, Luke 24:18. "Art thou only a stranger in Jerusalem, and hast not known the things which have come to pass there in these days;" plainly intimating, that the things concerning Jesus were so publicly known to all men, that it was wonderful to find any man unacquainted with them. And so afterwards they became acquainted with the news of his resurrection; and when they returned into their own countries, they carried the news with them, and made these facts public through the world, as before they had made the prophecies of them.

After this, those foreign Jews who came to Jerusalem, took great notice of the pouring out of the Spirit at Pentecost, and the wonderful effects of it; and many of them were converted by it. There were Parthians, Medes, Elamites, and the dwellers in Mesopotamia, and in Egypt, and the parts of Libya about Cyrene, and the strangers of Rome, Jews and proselytes, Cretes and Arabians. And so they not only carried back the news of these facts, but Christianity itself, into their own countries with them; which contributed much to the spreading of it through the world.

Again, the dispersion of the Jews opened a door for the introduction of the apostles in all places where they came to preach the gospel. For almost in all places where they came to preach the gospel, they found synagogues of the Jews, where the Holy Scriptures were wont to be read, and the true God worshipped; which was a great advantage to the apostles in spreading the gospel through the world. For their way was, into whatever city they came, first to go into the synagogue of the Jews, (they being of the same nation,) and there to preach the gospel unto them. And hereby their new doctrine was taken notice of by their Gentile neighbours, whose curiosity excited them to hear what they had to say; which became a fair occasion to the apostles to preach the gospel to them. This is the account we have in the Acts of the Apostles. And these Gentiles had been before, many of them, prepared in some measure, by the knowledge they had of the Jewish religion, of their worship of one God, their prophecies, and expectation of a Messiah. This knowledge they derived from the Jews, who had long been their neighbours; which opened the door for the gospel to have access to them. And the work of the apostles with them was doubtless much easier, than if they never had heard any thing before of such a person as the apostles preached, or any thing about the worship of one only true God. So many ways did the Babylonish captivity greatly prepare the way for Christ's coming.

**II.** The next particular that I would notice is, the addition made to the canon of Scripture in the time of the captivity, in those two remarkable portions of Scripture, the prophecies of Ezekiel and Daniel. Christ appeared to each of these prophets in the form of that nature which he was afterwards to take upon him. The prophet Ezekiel gives an account of his thus appearing to him repeatedly, as Ezek. 1:26. "And above the firmament that was over their heads, was the likeness of a throne, as the appearance of a sapphire-stone, and upon the likeness of the throne was the likeness as the appearance of a man above upon it;" and so Ezek. 8:1-2. So Christ appeared to the prophet Daniel: Dan. 8:15-16. "There stood before me as the appearance of a man. And I heard a man's voice between the banks of Ulai, which called, and said, Gabriel, make this man to understand the vision." There are several things which make it evident, that this was Christ; but I cannot now stand to mention particulars. Christ appeared as a man to this prophet, Dan. 10:5-6.

> Then I lift up mine eyes and looked, and behold, a certain man clothed in linen, whose loins were girded with fine gold of Uphaz: his body also was like the beryl, and his face as the appearance of lightning, and his eyes as lamps of fire, and his arms and his feet like in colour to polished brass, and the voice of his words like the voice of a multitude.

Comparing this vision with that of the apostle John in the 1st chapter of Revelation, makes it manifest that this person was Christ. And the prophet Daniel, in the historical part of his book, gives an account of a very remarkable appearance of Christ in Nebuchadnezzar's furnace, with Shadrach, Meshach, and Abednego. Dan. 3: 25. "Lo, I see four MEN loose,—and the form of the fourth is like the Son of God."

Christ not only appeared here in the form of the human nature, but he appeared in a furnace, saving those persons who believed on him from that furnace; by which is represented to us, how Christ, by coming himself into the furnace of God's wrath, saves those that believe in him from that furnace, so that it has no power on them; and the wrath of God never reaches or touches them, so much as to singe the hair of their head.

These two prophets, in many respects, were more particular concerning the coming of Christ, and his glorious gospel-kingdom, than any of the prophets had been before. They mention those three great overturnings of the world that should be before he came. Ezekiel is particular in several places concerning the coming of Christ. The prophet Daniel is more particular in foretelling the time of Christ's coming than ever any prophet had been before, (Dan. chap. 9) He foretold, that it should be seventy weeks, i.e. seventy weeks of years, or seventy times seven years, which is four hundred and ninety years, from the decree to rebuild and restore the state of the Jews, till the Messiah should be crucified. This must be reckoned from the commission given to Ezra by Artaxerxes, whereby the very particular time of Christ's crucifixion was pointed out, which never had been before. ( Ezra 7.)

The prophet Ezekiel is very particular in the mystical description of the gospel-church, in his vision of the temple and city, towards the latter part of his prophecy. The prophet Daniel points out the order of particular events that should come to pass relating to the Christian church after Christ was come, as the rise of Antichrist, the continuance of his reign, his fall, and the glory that should follow.—Thus does the gospel-light still increase, the nearer we come to the time of Christ's birth.

**III.** The next particular I would mention is, the destruction of Babylon, and the overthrow of the Chaldean empire by Cyrus. The destruction of Babylon took place on that night in which Belshazzar the king, and the city in general, were drowned in a drunken festival, which they kept in honour of their gods, when Daniel was called to read the hand-writing on the wall, Dan. 5:30. and it was brought about in such a manner, as wonderfully to show the hand of God, and remarkably to fulfil his word by his prophets, which I cannot now stand particularly to relate. Now that great city, which had long been an enemy to the city of God, was destroyed, after it had stood ever since the first building of Babel, which was about seventeen hundred years. If the check which was put to the building of this city at its beginning, whereby they were prevented from carrying it to that extent and magnificence they intended, promoted the work of redemption, much more did this destruction of it.

This was a remarkable instance of God's vengeance on the enemies of his redeemed church; for God brought destruction on Babylon for the injuries they did to God's children, as is often set forth in the prophets. It also promoted the work of redemption, as thereby God's people who were held captive by them, were set at liberty to return to their own land in order to rebuild Jerusalem; and therefore Cyrus is called God's shepherd, Isa. 14. And 15. And these are over and above those ways wherein the setting up and overthrowing the four monarchies of the world did promote the work of redemption.

**IV.** What next followed was the return of the Jews to their own land, and the rebuilding of Jerusalem and the temple. Cyrus, as soon as he had destroyed the Babylonish, and erected the Persian empire on its ruins, made a decree in favour of the Jews, that they might return to their own land, and rebuild their city and temple. This return of the Jews out of the Babylonish captivity is, next to the redemption out of Egypt, the most remarkable of all the Old-Testament redemptions, and most insisted on in Scripture, as a type of the great redemption of Jesus Christ. It was under the hand of one of the legal ancestors of Christ, viz. Zerubbabel, the son of Shealtiel, whose Babylonish name was Sheshbazzar. He was the governor of the Jews, and their leader in their first return out of captivity; and, together with Joshua the son of Josedek the high priest, had the chief hand in rebuilding the temple. This redemption was brought about by the hand of Zerubbabel and Joshua the priest, as the redemption out of Egypt was brought about by the hand of Moses and Aaron.

The return out of the captivity was a remarkable dispensation of Providence. It was remarkable, that the heart of a heathen prince, Cyrus, should be so inclined to favour such a design. He not only gave the people liberty to return, and rebuild the city and temple, but gave charge that they should be helped with silver and gold, with goods, and beasts, as we read in Ezra 1:4. And afterwards God wonderfully inclined the heart of Darius to further the building of the house of God with his own tribute-money, and gave command to their bitter enemies, the Samaritans, who had been striving to hinder them, to help them without fail, by furnishing them with all that they needed in order to it, and to supply them day by day. He made a decree, that whosoever failed of it, timber should be pulled down out of his house, and he hanged thereon, and his house made a dunghill, (Ezra 6) After this, God inclined the heart of Artaxerxes, another king of Persia, to promote the work of preserving the state of the Jews, by his ample commission to Ezra, (Ezra 7) He helped them abundantly with silver and gold out of his own bounty, and offered more, as should be needful, out of the king's treasure-house, commanding his treasurers beyond the river Euphrates to give more, as should be needed, unto a hundred talents of silver, a hundred measures of wheat, a hundred baths of wine, a hundred baths of oil, and salt, without prescribing how much. He gave leave to establish magistrates in the land; freeing the priests of toll, tribute, custom, and other things, which render this decree by Artaxerxes the most full and ample in the Jews' favour of any that had been given for the restoring of Jerusalem; and therefore, in Daniel's prophecy, this is called the decree for restoring and building Jerusalem; and hence the seventy weeks are dated.

After this, another favourable commission was granted by the king of Persia to Nehemiah, ( Nehemiah. chap. 2.)—It was remarkable, that the hearts of heathen princes should be so inclined. It was the effect of his power, who hath the hearts of kings in his hands, and turneth them whithersoever he will; and it was a remarkable instance of his favour to his people.

Another remarkable circumstance of this restitution of the state of the Jews to their own land was, that it was accomplished against so much opposition of their bitter indefatigable enemies, the Samaritans, who, for a long time together, with all the malice and craft they could exercise, opposed the Jews in this affair, and sought their destruction. One while they were opposed by Bishlam, Mithridath, Tabeel, Rehum, and Shimshai, as in Ezra 4 and then by Tatnai, Shetharboznai, and their companions, as in Ezra 5 and afterwards by Sunballat and Tobiah, as we read in the book of Nehemiah.

We have showed before, how the settlement of the people in this land in Joshua's time promoted the work of redemption. On the same accounts does their restitution belong to the same work. The re-settlement of the Jews in the land of Canaan belongs to this work, as it was a necessary means of preserving the Jewish church and dispensation in being, till Christ should come. If it had not been for this restoration of the Jewish church, temple, and worship, the people had remained without any temple, or land of their own, that should be as it were their headquarters, a place of worship, habitation, and resort. The whole constitution, which God had done so much to establish, would have been in danger of utterly failing, long before the six hundred years had expired, which was from about the time of the captivity till Christ. And so all that preparation which God had been making for the coming of Christ, from the time of Abraham, would have been in vain. Now that very temple was built that God would fill with glory by Christ's coming into it, as the prophets Haggai and Zechariah told the Jews in order to encourage them in building it.

**V.** The next particular I would observe, is the addition made to the canon of the Scriptures soon after the captivity by the prophets Haggai and Zechariah, who were prophets sent to encourage the people in their work of rebuilding the city and temple; and the main argument they use to that end, is the approach of the coming of Christ. Haggai foretold that Christ should be of Zerubbabel's legal posterity. This seems to be the last and most particular revelation of the descent of Christ, till the angel Gabriel was sent to reveal it to his mother Mary.

**VI.** The next thing I would take notice of, was the pouring out of the Spirit of God that accompanied the ministry of Ezra the priest after the captivity. That there was such an effusion of the Spirit of God, that accompanied Ezra's ministry, is manifest by many things in the books of Ezra and Nehemiah. Presently after Ezra came up from Babylon, with the ample commission which Artaxerxes gave him, whence Daniel's seventy weeks began, he set himself to reform the vices and corruptions he found among the Jews; and his great success in it we have an account of in the 10th chapter of Ezra. So that there appeared a very general and great mourning of the congregation of Israel for their sins, which was accompanied with a solemn covenant that the people entered into with God; and this was followed with a great and general reformation, as we have there an account. And the people about the same time, with great zeal, earnestness, and reverence, gathered themselves together to hear the word of God read by Ezra; and gave diligent attention, while Ezra and the other priests preached to them, by reading and expounding the law, and were greatly affected in the hearing of it. They wept when they heard the words of the law, and set themselves to observe it, and kept the feast of tabernacles, as the Scripture observes, after such a manner as it had not been kept since the days of Joshua the son of Nun,(Neh. 8.) After this, having separated themselves from all strangers, they solemnly observed a fast, by hearing the word, confessing their sins, and renewing their covenant with God. And they manifested their sincerity in that transaction, by actually reforming many abuses in religion and morals; as we learn from the 9th and following chapters of Nehemiah.

It is observable, that it has been God's manner, on every remarkable new establishment of the state of his visible church, to afford a remarkable outpouring of his

Spirit. So it was on the first establishment of the church of the Jews at their coming into Canaan under Joshua; so it was now in this second settlement of the church in the time of Ezra; and so it was on the first establishment of the Christian church after Christ's resurrection; God wisely and graciously laying the foundation of those establishments in a work of the Holy Spirit, for the lasting benefit of his church, thenceforward continued in those establishments. And this pouring out of the Spirit, was a final cure of the nation of that particular sin which just before they especially run into, viz. intermarrying with the Gentiles: for however inclined to it they were before, they ever after showed an aversion to it.

**VII.** Ezra added to the canon of the Scriptures. He wrote the book of Ezra; and he is supposed to have written the two books of Chronicles, at least of compiling them, if he was not the author of the materials, or all the parts, of these writings. That these books were written, or compiled and completed, after the captivity, the things contained in the books themselves make manifest; for the genealogies contained therein, are brought down below the captivity; as 1 Chron. 3:17, &c We have there an account of the posterity of Jehoiachin for several successive generations. And there is mention in these books of this captivity into Babylon, as of a thing past, and of things that were done on the return of the Jews after the captivity, (1 Chron. 9. ) The chapter is mostly filled up with an account of things that came to pass after the captivity into Babylon, as you may see by comparing it with what is said in the books of Ezra and Nehemiah. And that Ezra was the person who compiled these books, is probable by this, because they conclude with words that we know are the words of Ezra's history. The two last verses are Ezra's words in the history he gives in the two first verses of the book of Ezra.

**VIII.** Ezra is supposed to have collected all the books of which the Holy Scriptures did then consist, and disposed them in their proper order. Ezra is often spoken of as a noted and eminent scribe of the law of God, and the canon of Scripture in his time was manifestly under his special care. The Jews, from the first accounts we have from them, have always held, that the canon of Scripture, so much of it as was then extant, was collected, and orderly disposed and settled, by Ezra; and that from him they have delivered it down in the order in which he disposed it, till Christ's time; when the Christian church received it from them, and have delivered it down to our times. The truth of this is allowed as undoubted by divines in general.

**IX.** The work of redemption was carried on and promoted in this period, by greatly multiplying the copies of the law, and appointing the constant public reading of them in all the cities of Israel in their synagogues. It is evident, that before the captivity, there were but few copies of the law. The original was laid up beside the ark; and the kings were required to write out a copy of it for their use, and the law was required to be read to the whole congregation of Israel once every seventh year. And we have no account of any other stated public reading of the law before the captivity but this. And it is manifest by several things that might be mentioned, that copies of the law were exceeding rare before the captivity. But after this, the constant reading of the law was set up in every synagogue throughout the land. First, they began with reading the law, and then they proceeded to establish the constant reading of the other books of the Old Testament. And lessons were read out of the Old Testament, as made up of both the law and the other parts of the Scripture then extant, in all the synagogues, which were set up in every city, and wherever the Jews in any considerable number dwelt. Thus we find it was in the time of Christ and the apostles. Acts 15:21. "Moses of old time hath in every city them that preach him, being read in the synagogues every sabbath-day." This custom is universally supposed, both by Jews and Christians, to be begun by Ezra. There were doubtless public assemblies before the captivity. They used to assemble at the temple at their great feasts, and were directed, when they were at a loss about any thing in the law, to go to the priest for instruction; and they used also to resort to the prophets' houses: and we read of synagogues in the land before, Psalm 74:8. But it is not supposed that they had copies of the law for constant public reading and expounding through the land before. This was one great means of their being preserved from idolatry.

**X.** The next thing I would mention, is God's remarkably preserving the church and nation of the Jews, when they were in imminent danger of being universally destroyed by Haman, as in the book of Esther. This series of providence was very wonderful in preventing this destruction. Esther was doubtless born for this end, to be the instrument of this remarkable preservation.

**XI.** After this the canon of Scripture was further enlarged in the books of Nehemiah and Esther; the one by Nehemiah himself. Whether the other was written by Nehemiah, or Mordecai, or Malachi, is not of importance for us to know, so long as it is one of those books that were always admitted and received as a part of their canon by the Jews, and was among those books which the Jews called their Scriptures in Christ's time, and as such was approved by him. For Christ often in his speeches to the Jews, manifestly approves and confirms those books, which amongst them went by the name of the Scriptures, as might easily be shown.

**XII.** After this the canon of the Old Testament was completed and sealed by Malachi. The manner of his concluding his prophecy seems to imply, that they were to expect no more prophecies, and no more written revelations from God, till Christ should come. For in the last chapter he prophesies of Christ's coming; Malachi 4:2-3.

> But unto you that fear my name, shall the Sun of righteousness arise with healing in his wings; and ye shall go forth and grow up as calves of the stall. And ye shall tread down the wicked; for they shall be as ashes under

the soles of your feet, in the day that I shall do this, saith the Lord of hosts.

Then we read in Malachi 4:4. "Remember ye the law of Moses my servant, which I commanded unto him in Horeb for all Israel, with the statutes and judgments," i.e. Remember and improve what ye have; keep close to your written rule, as expecting no more additions to it, till the night of the Old Testament is over, and the Sun of righteousness shall at length arise.

**XIII.** Soon after this, the spirit of prophecy ceased among that people till the time of the New Testament. Thus the Old-Testament light, the stars of the long night, began apace to hide their heads, the time of the Sun of righteousness now drawing nigh. We before observed, how the kings of the house of David ceased before the true king and head of the church came; and how the cloud of glory withdrew, before Christ, the brightness of the Father's glory, appeared. And now the spirit of prophecy ceased. The time of the great prophet of God was now so nigh, it was time for their typical prophets to be silent.

We have now gone through the time of which we have any historical account in the writings of the Old Testament; and the last thing mentioned, by which the work of redemption was promoted, was the ceasing of the spirit of prophecy.—I now proceed to show how the work of redemption was carried on through the remaining times before Christ. In this we have not that thread of scripture history to guide us that we have had

hitherto; but have these three things, viz. the prophecies of the Old Testament, human histories, and some
occasional evidence of things which happened in those
times, in the New Testament. Therefore,

**XIV.** The next particular that I shall mention under
this period, is the destruction of the Persian empire,
and setting up of the Grecian empire by Alexander.
This came to pass about sixty or seventy years after
the times wherein the prophet Malachi is supposed to
have prophesied, and about three hundred and thirty years before Christ. This was the third revolution
that came to pass in this period, and was greater and
more remarkable than either of the foregoing. It was
very remarkable on account of the suddenness of that
conquest which Alexander made, and the greatness of
the empire he set up, which much exceeded in extent
all the foregoing.

This event is much spoken of in the prophecies of
Daniel. This empire is represented by the third kingdom
of brass in Daniel's interpretation of Nebuchadnezzar's
dream, Dan. 2. And in Daniel's vision of the four beasts,
it is represented by the third beast that was like a leopard,
that had on his back four wings of a fowl, to represent the swiftness of its conquest, Dan. 7. and is more
particularly represented by the he-goat in Dan. 8, that
came from the west on the face of the whole earth,
and touched not the ground, to represent how swiftly
Alexander overran the world. The angel himself expressly
interprets this he-goat to signify the king of Grecia, Dan.

8:21. "The rough goat is the king of Grecia; and the great horn that is between his eyes is the first king," i.e. Alexander himself.

After Alexander had conquered the world, he soon died; and his dominion did not descend to his posterity, but four of his principal captains divided his empire between them. Now that being broken, and four stood up for it, four kingdoms stand up out of the nation, but not in his power; as in the 11th chapter of Daniel. The angel after foretelling the Persian empire, proceeds to foretell Alexander, Dan. 11: 3. "And a mighty king shall stand up, that shall rule with great dominion, and do according to his will." Then he foretells, in the 4th verse, the dividing of his kingdom between his four captains: Dan. 11:4. "And when he shall stand up, his kingdom shall be broken, and shall be divided toward the four winds of heaven; and not to his posterity, nor according to his dominion which he ruled: for his kingdom shall be plucked up, even for others besides those. Of these four captains, one had Egypt and the neighbouring countries on the south of Judea; and another had Syria and the neighbouring countries north of Judea; and these two are called the kings of the north and of the south. (Dan. 11. )

Now, this setting up of the Grecian empire did greatly prepare the way for Christ's coming, and for the erection of his kingdom. Besides the ways common to others in this period, there is one peculiar to this revolution, which remarkably promoted the work of redemption; and that was, that it made the Greek language common in the world. To have one common language understood and used through the greater part of the world, must greatly prepare the way for the setting up of Christ's kingdom. This gave advantage for spreading the gospel through all nations, with vastly greater ease, than if every nation had a distinct language, and did not understand each other. For though some of the first preachers of the gospel had the gift of tongues, so that they could preach in any language; yet all had not this particular gift; and they who had could not exercise it when they would, but only at special seasons, when the Spirit of God was pleased to inspire them in this way. And the churches in different and distant parts of the world, as at Jerusalem, Antioch, Galatia, Corinth, &c. could not have had that communication of which we have an account in the book of Acts, without a common language.—After the Grecian empire was set up, many in all these countries well understood the Greek language; which wonderfully opened the door for mutual communication between those churches which were so far separated one from another.

Again, making the Greek language common through so great a part of the world, did wonderfully make way for the kingdom of Christ, because it was the language in which the New Testament was to be originally written. The apostles propagated the gospel through many scores of nations; and if those nations could not have understood the Bible any otherwise than as it was translated into so many languages, it would have rendered the spreading of the gospel vastly more difficult. But by the

Greek being made common to all, they all understood the New Testament of Jesus Christ in the language in which the apostles and evangelists originally wrote it. As soon as ever it was written by its original penmen, it immediately lay open to the world in a language that was commonly understood.

**XV.** The next thing I notice is the translating of the Old Testament into the Greek language, which was commonly understood by the Gentiles. This is commonly called the Septuagint, or the translation of the Seventy; and is supposed to have been made about fifty or sixty years after Alexander's conquests. This is the first translation that ever was made of the Scriptures that we have any credible account of. The canon of the Old Testament had been completed by the prophet Malachi but about a hundred and twenty years before in its original. Hitherto the Scriptures had remained locked up among the Jews in the Hebrew tongue, which was understood by no other nation; but now it was translated into a language that was commonly understood by the nations of the world.

This translation of the Old Testament is still extant, and is of great use. The Jews have many fables about the occasion and manner of this translation; but the truth of the case is supposed to be this, that multitudes of the Jews living in other parts of the world besides Judea, and being born and bred among the Greeks, the Greek became their common language. These not understanding the original Hebrew, they procured the Scriptures to be translated for their use into the Greek language: and so henceforward the Jews, in all countries, except Judea, were wont in their synagogues to make use of this translation instead of the Hebrew.

This translation of the Scriptures into a language so commonly understood through the world, greatly prepared the way for setting up Christ's kingdom in the world. For the apostles commissioned to preach through the world, made great use of the scriptures of the Old Testament, and especially of the prophecies concerning Christ that were contained in them. By means of this translation, and by the Jews being scattered every where, they had the Scriptures at hand in a language understood by the Gentiles. Hence they principally made use of this translation in their preaching and writings wherever they went. In all the numerous quotations out of the Old Testament in their writings, they are made almost every where in the very words of the Septuagint. The sense is the same as in the original Hebrew; though the words are different. But yet this makes it evident, that the apostles in their preaching and writings, commonly made use of this translation. And this translation was principally used in Christian churches through most nations of the world, for several hundred years after Christ.

**XVI.** The next thing is the wonderful preservation of the church when it was eminently threatened and persecuted under the Grecian empire. The first time they were threatened was by Alexander himself. When besieging the city of Tyre, he sent to the Jews for assistance and supplies for his army. Out of a conscientious regard to their oath to the king of Persia, they refused; but he being a man of a very furious spirit, agreeable to the scripture representation of the rough he-goat, marched against them, with a design to cut them off. When he met the priests going out to him in their priestly garments, God wonderfully turned his heart to spare them, and favour them, as he did the heart of Esau when he met Jacob.

After this, one of the kings of Egypt, a successor of one of Alexander's four captains, entertained a design of destroying the nation of the Jews; but was remarkably and wonderfully prevented by a stronger interposition of Heaven for their preservation.

But the most wonderful preservation of them all in this period was under the cruel persecution of Antiochus Epiphanes, king of Syria, and successor of another of Alexander's four captains. The Jews were at that time subject to the power of Antiochus; and he being enraged against them, long strove to his utmost utterly to destroy them, and root them out; at least all of them that would not forsake their religion, and worship his idols. He did indeed in a great measure waste the country, and depopulate the city of Jerusalem; and profaned the temple, by setting up his idols in some parts of it; and persecuted the people with insatiable cruelty; so that we have no account of any persecution like this before. Many of the particular circumstances of this persecution would be very affecting were there time to insist on them. This cruel persecution began about a hundred and seventy years before Christ. It is spoken of in the prophecy of Daniel, Dan. 8: 9, 25. 11:31-38. and in the New Testament, Heb. 11:36-38.

Antiochus intended not only to extirpate the Jewish religion, but, as far as in him lay, the very nation; and particularly laboured to the utmost to destroy all copies of the law. And considering how weak they were, in comparison with a king of such vast dominion, the providence of God appears very wonderful in defeating his design. Many times the Jews seemed to be on the very brink of ruin, just ready to be wholly swallowed up; and their enemies often thought themselves sure of obtaining their purpose. They once came against the people with a mighty army, with a design of killing all, except the women and children, and of selling these for slaves; and so confident were they of obtaining their purpose, and others of purchasing, that above a thousand merchants came with the army, with money in their hands, to buy the slaves that should be sold. But God wonderfully stirred up and assisted one Judas, and others his successors, called the Maccabees, who, with a small handful in comparison vanquished their enemies time after time, and delivered their nation. This also was foretold by Daniel, Speaking of Antiochus's persecution, he says, Daniel 11:32. "And such as do wickedly against the covenant, shall be corrupt by flatteries: but the people that do know their God, shall be strong and do exploits."

God afterwards brought this Antiochus to a fearful, miserable end, by a loathsome disease, under dreadful torments of body and horrors of mind; which was foretold, in these words, (Dan. 11: 45.)" Yet he shall come to his end, and none shall help him." After his death, there were attempts still to destroy the church; but God baffled them all.

**XVII.** The next thing is the destruction of the Grecian, and setting up of the Roman, empire. This was the fourth revolution in this period. And though it was brought to pass more gradually than the setting up of the Grecian empire, yet it far exceeded that, and was much the greatest and largest temporal monarchy that ever was in the world; so that the Roman empire was commonly called all the world; as in Luke 2:1. "And there went out a decree from Caesar Augustus, that all the world should be taxed:" i.e. all the Roman empire.

This empire is spoken of as much the strongest and greatest of any of the four: Dan. 2:40. "And the fourth kingdom shall be strong as iron: forasmuch as iron breaketh in pieces, and subdueth all things: and as iron that breaketh all these, shall it break in pieces, and bruise." Dan. 7:7, 19, 23. The time when the Romans first conquered and subdued the land of Judea, was between sixty and seventy years before Christ. Soon after this, the Roman empire was established in its greatest extent; and the world continued subject to it henceforward till Christ came, and many hundred years after.

The nations being thus united under one monarchy when Christ came, and when the apostles went forth to preach the gospel, greatly prepared the way for the spreading of the gospel, and the setting up of

Christ's kingdom in the world.—For the world being thus subject to one government, it opened a general communication, and so opportunity was given for the more swift propagation of the gospel. Thus we find it in the British dominions, the communication is quick from one part to another. There are innumerable difficulties in travelling through different nations, that are under different independent governments, which there are not in travelling through different parts of the same realm, or different dominions of the same prince. So the world being under one government, that of the Romans, facilitated the apostles' travelling.

**XVIII.** About the same time learning and philosophy were risen to their greatest height in the heathen world.—Almost all the famous philosophers among the heathen, were after the captivity into Babylon. Almost all the wise men of Greece and Rome flourished in this time. What these philosophers in general chiefly professed as their business, was to inquire, wherein man's chief happiness lay, and how to obtain it. They seemed earnestly to busy themselves in this inquiry, and wrote multitudes of books about it, many of which are still extant; but they were exceedingly divided, there having been reckoned several hundreds of different opinions which they had concerning it. Thus they wearied themselves in vain, wandering in the dark, not having the glorious gospel to guide them. God was pleased to suffer men to do the utmost that they could with human wisdom, and to try the utmost extent of their own understandings in order to find out the way to happiness, before the true light came to enlighten the world. God suffered these great philosophers to try what they could do for six hundred years together; and then it proved by the events of so long a time, that all they could do was in vain; the world not becoming wiser, better, or happier under their instructions, but growing more and more foolish, wicked, and miserable. He suffered this, that it might be seen how far reason and philosophy could go in their highest ascent, that the necessity of a divine teacher might more convincingly appear. God was pleased to make foolish the wisdom of this world—to show men the folly of their best wisdom—by the doctrines of his glorious gospel, which were above the reach of all their philosophy. See 1 Cor. 1:19-21.

After God had showed the vanity of human learning, when set up in the room of the gospel, God was pleased to make it subservient to the purposes of Christ's kingdom, as a handmaid to divine revelation. Thereby the vanity of human wisdom was shown, and the necessity of the gospel appeared; and hereby a handmaid was prepared to the gospel. An instance of this we have in the apostle Paul, who was famed for his much learning, (Acts 26:24. ) being skilled in the learning not only of the Jews, but also of the philosophers. This he improved to subserve the gospel; as he did in disputing with the philosophers at Athens, Acts 17:22, &c. By his learning he knew how to accommodate himself in his discourses to learned men, having read their writings; and he cites their own poets. Dionysius, a philosopher, was converted by him, and was made a great instrument of promoting the gospel. And there were many others in that and the following ages, who were eminently useful by their human learning in promoting the interests of Christ's kingdom.

**XIX.** Just before Christ was born, the Roman empire was raised to its greatest height, and also settled in peace. About four and twenty years before Christ, Augustus Caesar, the first Roman emperor, began to rule as emperor of the world. Till then the Roman empire had of a long time been a commonwealth under the government of the senate: but then it became an absolute monarchy. This personage, as he was the first, so he was the greatest of all the Roman emperors: he reigned in the greatest glory. Thus the power of the heathen world, which was Satan's visible kingdom, was raised to its greatest height, after it had been strengthening itself more and more from the days of Solomon, which was about a thousand years. Now the heathen world was in its greatest glory for strength, wealth, and learning.

God did two things to prepare the way for Christ's coming, wherein he took a contrary method from that which human wisdom would have taken. He brought his own visible people very low, and made them weak; but the heathen, his enemies, he exalted to the greatest height, for the more glorious triumph of the cross of Christ. With a small number in their greatest weakness, he conquered his enemies in their greatest glory. Thus

Christ triumphed over principalities and powers in his cross.

Augustus Caesar had been for many years establishing his empire, and subduing his enemies, till the very year that Christ was born: when, all his enemies being subdued, his dominion over the world seemed to be gloriously settled. All was established in peace; in token whereof the Romans shut the temple of Janus, which was an established symbol among them of there being universal peace throughout the empire. And this universal peace, which was begun that very year in which Christ was born, lasted twelve years, even till the year that Christ disputed with the doctors in the temple.

Thus the world, after it had been, as it were, in a continual convulsion for so many hundred years together—like the four winds striving together on the tumultuous raging ocean, whence arose those four great monarchies—was now established in the greatest height of the fourth and last monarchy, and settled in quietness. Now all things are ready for the birth of Christ. This remarkable universal peace, after so many ages of tumult and war, was a fit prelude for ushering the glorious Prince of peace into the world.

Thus I have gone through the first grand period of the whole space between the fall of man and the end of the world, viz. from the fall to the time of the incarnation of Christ; and have shown the truth of the first proposition, viz. That from the fall of man to the incarnation of Christ, God was doing those things which were preparatory to Christ's coming, and were forerunners of it.

## 1.7 PART VII

### 7.0 Improvement of the First Period

BEFORE I PROCEED to the next period, I would make some few remarks, by way of improvement upon what has been said under this.

**I.** From what has been said, we may strongly argue, that Jesus of Nazareth is indeed the Son of God, and the Saviour of the world; and so that the Christian religion is the true religion, seeing that Christ is the very person so evidently pointed at, in all the great dispensations of Divine Providence from the very fall of man, and was so undoubtedly in so many instances foretold from age to age, and shadowed forth in a vast variety of types and figures. If we seriously consider the course of things from the beginning, and observe the motions of all the great wheels of providence, we shall discern that they all tend hither. They are all as so many lines, whose course, if it be observed and accurately followed, will be found to centre here. It is so very plain in many things, that it would argue stupidity to deny it. This person, sent from God, came into the world with his commission and authority, to do his work, and to declare his mind. The Governor of the world, in all his great works towards Jews and Gentiles, down to the time of Christ's birth, has declared it. It is a plain and evident truth, that he who was born at Bethlehem, who dwelt at Nazareth and Capernaum, and who was crucified without the gates of Jerusalem, must be the great Messiah. Blessed are all they that believe in and confess him, and miserable are all that deny him. This shows the unreasonableness of the deists, who deny revealed religion, and of the Jews, who deny that this Jesus is the Messiah foretold and promised to their fathers.

Here should any object, That it may be, some cunning men contrived this history, and these prophecies, on purpose to prove that he is the Messiah. To such it may be replied, How could such a thing be contrived by cunning men to point to Jesus Christ, long before he ever was born? How could they know that any such person would be born? And how could their subtlety help them to foresee and point at an event that was to come to pass many ages afterwards? For no fact can be more evident, than that the Jews had those writings long before Christ was born: as they have them still in great veneration, in all their dispersions through the world. They would never have received such a contrivance from Christians, to prove Jesus to be the Messiah, whom they always denied; and much less would they have been made to believe that they always had those books in their hands, if they had been an imposition.

**II.** What has been said, affords a strong argument for the divine authority of the books of the Old Testament, from that admirable harmony there is in them, whereby they all point to the same thing. For we may see by what has been said, how all the parts of the Old Testament, though written by so many different penmen, and in ages so distant, harmonize one with another. All agree in one, and centre in the same event; which it was impossible for any one of them to know, but by divine revelation.

Now, if the Old Testament was not inspired by God, what account can be given of such an agreement? For if these books were written without any divine direction, then none of these penmen knew that there would come such a person as Jesus Christ into the world; his coming was only a mere figment of their own brain: and if so, how happened it, that this figment of theirs came to pass ? How came a vain imagination of theirs, which they foretold without any manner of ground for their prediction, to be exactly fulfilled? and especially how did they come all to agree in it, all pointing exactly to the same thing, though many of them lived so many hundred years distant one from another?—This admirable consent and agreement in a future event, is therefore a clear and certain evidence of the divine authority of those writings.

**III.** Hence we may learn how weak and ignorant the objection is, against the Old Testament being the word of God, because it consists so much of warlike histories and civil transactions. Here, say some, we have histories of their kings and rulers, their wars with neighbouring nations, and the changes that happened in their state and government: but other nations used to keep histories of their public affairs, as well as they; why then should we think that these histories which the Jews kept are the word of God, more than those of other people? What has been said, shows the folly and vanity of such an objection. For hereby it appears, that the case of these histories is very different from that of all others. This history alone gives us an account of the first original of all things; and this alone deduces things down to us in a wonderful series from that original, giving an idea of the grand scheme of Divine Providence, as tending to its great end. And, together with the doctrines and prophecies contained in it, the same book gives a view of the whole series of the great events of Divine Providence, from the origin to the consummation of all things; exhibiting an excellent and glorious account of the wise and holy designs of the supreme Governor in all.—No common history has had such penmen. This history was all written by men who came with evident signs and testimonies of their being prophets of the most high God, immediately inspired.—And though histories, yet containing those great events of providence by which it appears how God has been carrying on the glorious work of redemption from age to age, they are no less full of divine instruction, and those things that show forth Christ, and his glorious gospel, than the other parts of the Holy Scriptures.

To object against a book's being divine, merely because it is historical, is a poor fancy; as if that could not be the word of God which gives an account of what is past; or as though it were not reasonable to suppose, that God, in a revelation he should give mankind, would give us any relation of the dispensations of his own providence. If so, it must be because his works are not worthy to be related: or because the scheme of his government, and the series of his dispensations towards his church, and the world he has made, is not worthy that any record should be kept of it.

The objection, That it is a common thing for nations and kingdoms to write histories and keep records of their wars, and the revolutions that come to pass in their territories, is so far from being a weighty objection against the historical part of Scripture, as though it were not the word of God, that it is a strong argument in favour of it. For if the light of nature teaches all civilized nations to keep records of the events of their government and the series of their administrations, and to publish histories for the information of others, how much more may we expect that God would give the world a record of the dispensations of his government, which doubtless is infinitely more worthy of a history for our information? If wise kings have taken care that there should be good histories written of the nations over which they have reigned, shall we think it incredible, that Jesus Christ should take care that his church, which is his nation, his peculiar people, should have in their hands a certain infallible history of their nation, and of his government of them?

If it had not been for the history of the Old Testament, how woefully should we have been left in the dark about many things which the church of God needs to know! How ignorant should we have been of God's dealings towards mankind, and towards his church, from the beginning! We should have been wholly in the dark about the creation of the world, the fall of man, the first rise and continued progress of the dispensations of grace towards fallen mankind. We should have known nothing how God at first set up a church in the world, and how it was preserved; after what manner he governed it from the beginning; how the light of the gospel first began to dawn in the world; how it increased, and how things were preparing for the coining of Christ.

If we are Christians, we belong to that building of God that has been the subject of our discourse: but if it had not been for the history of the Old Testament, we should never have known what was the first occasion of God's going about this building, how the foundation of it was laid, and how it has gone on from the beginning. The times of the history of the Old Testament are mostly such as no other history includes; and therefore, if God had not taken care to give and preserve an account of these things for us, we should have been wholly without them.

Those that object against the authority of the Old-Testament history, may as well object against Moses's account of the creation; for, in the former, we have a history of a work no less important, viz. the work of redemption. Yea, this is a far greater and more glorious work. If it be inquired which of the two works, that of creation, or that of providence, is greatest? it must be answered, the work of providence; but the work of redemption is the greatest of the works of providence.— And let those who make this objection consider what part of the Old-Testament history can be spared, without making a great breach in that thread or series of events by which this glorious work has been carried on.—This leads me to observe,

**IV.** That, from what has been said, we may see much of the wisdom of God in the composition of the Scriptures of the Old Testament, i.e. in the parts of which it consists. Let us briefly take a view of the several parts of it, and of the need there was of them.

It was necessary, for instance, that we should have some account of the creation of the world, of our first parents, and their primitive state; of the fall, of the old world, and its degeneracy; of the universal deluge, and the origin of nations after this destruction of mankind.

It seems necessary, moreover, that there should be some account of the succession of the church of God from the beginning. God suffered all the world to degenerate, and took one nation only to be his people, to preserve the true worship and religion till the Saviour of the world should come. In them the world was gradually prepared for that great light, and those wonderful things of which he was to be the author. Thus they were a typical nation, that in them God might shadow forth and teach, as under a vail, all the future glories of the gospel. It was therefore necessary that we should have some account of this; how it was first effected by the call of Abraham, and by their being bond-slaves in Egypt, and how they were brought to Canaan. It was necessary that we should have some account of the revelation which

God made of himself to that people, in giving their law, in the appointment of their typical worship, wherein the gospel is vailed, and of the formation of their civil and ecclesiastical state.

It seems exceedingly necessary that we should have some account of their being actually brought to Canaan, the country promised them and where they always dwelt; that we should have a history of the successions of the church of Israel, and of those providences towards them, which were most considerable and fullest of gospel mystery; that we should have some account of the promised external glory of that nation under David and Solomon, and a very particular account of David, whose history is so full of the gospel, and in whom began the race of their kings; and that we should have some account of the building of the temple, which was also full of gospel-mystery.

And it is a matter of great consequence, that we should have some account of Israel's dividing from Judah, and of the ten tribes' captivity and utter rejection, and therefore a brief history of them till that time; that we should have an account of the succession of the kings of Judah, and of the church, till their captivity into Babylon; of their return from captivity, and resettlement in their own land, with the origin of the last state of the church before Christ came.

A little consideration will convince any one, that all these things were necessary, and that none of them could be spared; and in the general, that it was necessary we should have a history of God's church till such times as are within the reach of human histories. It was of vast importance that we should have an inspired history of those times of the Jewish church, wherein there was kept up a more extraordinary intercourse between God and them, while he used to dwell among them as it were visibly, revealing himself by the Shechinah, by Urim and Thummim, and by prophecy, and so more immediately to order their affairs. And it was necessary that we should have some account of the great dispensations of God in prophecy, after the finishing of inspired history; for which it was needful that there should be a number of prophets raised who should foretell the coming of the Son of God, and the nature and glory of his kingdom, as so many harbingers to make way for him, and that their prophecies should remain in the church.

It was also a matter of great consequence that the church should have a book of divine songs given by inspiration from God, wherein there should be a lively representation of the true spirit of devotion, of faith, hope, and divine love, of joy, resignation, humility, obedience, repentance, &c. as in the Psalms; also that we should have from God such books of moral instructions as we have in Proverbs and Ecclesiastes, relating to the affairs and state of mankind, and the concerns of human life, containing rules of true wisdom and prudence for our conduct in all circumstances; and that we should have particularly a song representing the great love between Christ and his spouse the church, adapted to the disposition and holy affections of a true Christian soul towards Christ, and representing his grace and marvelous love to, and delight in, his people, as in Solomon's Song. It is important that we should have a book to teach us how to conduct ourselves under affliction, seeing the church of God here is in a militant state, and God's people through much tribulation enter into the kingdom of heaven. The church is for a long time under trouble, meets with fiery trials, and extreme sufferings, before her time of peace and rest in the latter ages of the world. Therefore God has given us a book most proper in these circumstances, the book of Job; and though written on occasion of the afflictions of a particular saint, it was probably at first given to the church in Egypt under her afflictions there; and is made use of by the apostle to comfort Christians under persecutions, James 5:11. "Ye have heard of the patience of Job, and have seen the end of the Lord; that the Lord is very pitiful, and of tender mercy." God was also pleased, in this book of Job, to give some view of the ancient divinity before the giving of the law.

Thus, from this brief review, I think it appears, that every part of the scriptures of the Old Testament is very useful and necessary, and no part of it can be spared without loss to the church. And therefore the wisdom of God is conspicuous in ordering, that the scriptures of the Old Testament should consist of those very books of which they do consist.

Before I dismiss this particular, I would add, that it is very observable, that the history of the Old Testament is large and particular where the great affair of redemption required it; even where there was most done towards this work, most to typify Christ, and to prepare the way for him. Thus it is very particular in the history of Abraham and the other patriarchs; but very short in the account we have of the time which the children of Israel spent in Egypt. It is large in the account of the redemption out of Egypt, and the first settling of the affairs of the Jewish church and nation in the time of Moses and Joshua; but much shorter in the times of the judges. So again, it is large and particular in the times of David and Solomon, and then very short in the history of the ensuing reigns. Thus the accounts are large and short, just as there is more or less of the affair of redemption to be seen in them.

V. From what has been said, we may see, that Christ and his redemption are the great subject of the whole Bible. Concerning the New Testament, the matter is plain; and by what has been said, it appears to be so also with respect to the Old Testament. Christ and his redemption is the great subject of the prophecies of the Old Testament, as has been shown. It has also been shown, that he is the great subject of the songs of the Old Testament; and the moral rules and precepts are all given in subordination to him. Christ and his redemption are also the great subject of the history of the Old Testament from the beginning all along; and even the history of the creation is brought in as an introduction to the history of redemption that immediately follows it. The whole book, both Old Testament and New, is filled up with the gospel; only with this difference, that the Old Testament contains the gospel under a vail, but the New contains it unveiled, so that we may see the glory of the Lord with open face.

**VI.** By what has been said, we may see the usefulness and excellency of the Old Testament. Some are ready to look on the Old Testament as being out of date, and as if we in these days of the gospel have but little to do with it. But this is a very great mistake, arising from want of observing the nature and design of the Old Testament, which, if it were observed, would appear full of the gospel of Christ, and would in an excellent manner illustrate and confirm the glorious doctrines and promises of the New Testament. Those parts of the Old Testament which are commonly looked upon as containing the least divine instruction, are mines and treasures of gospel-knowledge; and the reason why they are thought to contain so little is, because persons do but superficially read them. The treasures which are hid underneath are not observed. They only look on the top of the ground, and suddenly pass a judgment that there is nothing there. But they never dig into the mine: if they did, they would find it richly stored with what is more valuable than silver and gold, and would be abundantly requited for their pains.

What has been said, may show us what a precious treasure God has committed into our hands, in that he has given us the Bible. How little do most persons consider what a privilege they enjoy, in the possession of that holy book, the Bible, which they have in their hands, and may converse with as they please. What an excellent book is this, and how far exceeding all human writings! It reveals God to us, and gives us a view of the grand design and glorious scheme of providence from the beginning of the world, either in history or prophecy. It reveals the great Redeemer, his glorious redemption, and the various steps by which God accomplishes it from the first foundation to the top-stone! Shall we prize a history which gives us a clear account of some great earthly prince, or mighty warrior, as of an Alexander, a Caesar, or a Marlborough? And shall we not prize the history that God gives us of the glorious kingdom of his Son Jesus Christ, the Prince and Saviour, and of the great transactions of that King of kings, and Lord of armies, the Lord mighty in battle; and what he has wrought for the redemption of his chosen people?

**VII.** What has been said, may make us sensible how much most persons are to blame for their inattentive, unobservant way of reading the Scriptures. How much profitable matter do the Scriptures contain, if it were but observed! The Bible is the most comprehensive book in the world. But what will all this signify to us, if we read it without observing what is the drift of the Holy Ghost in it? The psalmist, begs of God, Psalm 119:18. "That he would enlighten his eyes that he might behold wondrous things out of his law." The Scriptures are full of wondrous things. Those histories which are too commonly read as if they were only private concerns of particular persons, such as of Abraham, Isaac, Jacob, and Joseph; of Ruth, Joshua, the Judges, David and the Israelitish princes, are accounts of vastly greater things, things of greater importance and more extensive concernment, than they who read them are commonly aware of.

The histories of Scripture are but too commonly read, as if they were written only to entertain men's fancies, when the infinitely great things contained in them are passed over without notice. Whatever treasures the Scriptures contain, we shall be never the better for them if we do not observe them. He that has a Bible, and does not observe what it contains, is like a man who has a box full of silver and gold, and does not know it, nor observe that it is any thing more than a vessel filled with common stones. He will be never the better for his treasure; and so might as well be without it. He who has plenty of the choicest food stored up in his house, and does not know it, will never taste what he has, and will be as likely to starve as if his house were empty.

**VIII.** What has been said, may show us how great a person Jesus Christ is, and how great his errand into the world, seeing there was so much done to prepare the way for his coming. God had been preparing the way for him through all ages of the world from the very beginning. If we had notice of a certain stranger being about to come into a country, and should observe that a great preparation was made for him, great things were done, many alterations made in the state of the whole country, many hands employed, persons of great note engaged in making the preparation; and all the affairs and concerns of the country ordered so as to be subservient to the design of entertaining that person, it would be natural for us to think, surely this is some extraordinary person, and it is some very great business that he is coming upon. How great a person then must he be, for whose coming the great God of heaven and earth, and Governor of all things, spent four thousand years in preparing the way! Soon after the world was created, and from age to age, he has been doing great things, bringing mighty events to pass, accomplishing wonders without number, often overturning the world in order to it. He has been causing every thing in the state of mankind, and all revolutions and changes in the habitable world, from generation to generation, to be subservient to this great design.—Surely this must be some great and extraordinary person, and a great work indeed it must needs be, about which he is coming.

We read, (Matt. 21:8-10.) when Christ was coming into Jerusalem, and multitudes ran before him, having cut down branches of palm-trees, and strewed them in the way; and others spread their garments in the way, crying, " Hosanna to the Son of David," that the whole city was moved, saying, Who is this? They wondered who that extraordinary person should be, that there should be such preparation made on occasion of his coming into the city. But if we consider, what great things were done in all ages to prepare the way for Christ's coming, and how the world was often overturned to make way for it, much more may we cry out, Who is this? What great person is this? and say, (as in Psalm 24:8, 10.) "Who is this King of glory," that God should show such respect, and put such vast honour upon him? Surely this person is honourable in God's eyes, and greatly beloved of him; and surely it is a grand errand upon which he is sent.

# About the Contributor

Paul Aurich is a father, home educator, and independent researcher. His research interests include church history, cultural philosophy, apologetics, worldview studies, and biblical exegesis. He holds a Bachelor of Religious Studies from Heritage College and Seminary and a Master of Theological Studies from McMaster Divinity College.

Paul resides in Grimsby, Ontario with his loving wife Karen and his six children, Nathanael, Tobias, Liza, Josiah, Seth, and Isaiah.

www.ingramcontent.com/pod-product-compliance
Lightning Source LLC
Chambersburg PA
CBHW021615120626
46545CB00001B/236

*9 7 8 1 9 9 0 7 7 1 8 1 1*